APOCALYPSE WHEN?

APOCALYPSE WHEN?

A Guide to Interpreting and Preaching Apocalyptic Texts

By LEAH D. SCHADE
and JERRY L. SUMNEY

CASCADE *Books* • Eugene, Oregon

APOCALYPSE WHEN?
A Guide to Interpreting and Preaching Apocalyptic Texts

Copyright © 2020 Leah D. Schade and Jerry L. Sumney. All rights reserved. Except for brief quotations in critical publications or reviews, no part of this book may be reproduced in any manner without prior written permission from the publisher. Write: Permissions, Wipf and Stock Publishers, 199 W. 8th Ave., Suite 3, Eugene, OR 97401.

Cascade Books
An Imprint of Wipf and Stock Publishers
199 W. 8th Ave., Suite 3
Eugene, OR 97401

www.wipfandstock.com

PAPERBACK ISBN: 978-1-7252-6247-8
HARDCOVER ISBN: 978-1-7252-6248-5
EBOOK ISBN: 978-1-7252-6249-2

Cataloguing-in-Publication data:

Names: Schade, Leah D., author. | Sumney, Jerry L., author.

Title: Apocalypse when? : interpreting and preaching apocalyptic texts / Leah D. Schade and Jerry L. Sumney.

Description: Eugene, OR: Cascade Books, 2020 | Includes bibliographical references.

Identifiers: ISBN 978-1-7252-6247-8 (paperback) | ISBN 978-1-7252-6248-5 (hardcover) | ISBN 978-1-7252-6249-2 (ebook)

Subjects: LCSH: Bible—Homiletical use. | Apocalyptic literature.

Classification: BS646 .A636 2020 (print) | BS646 (ebook)

Manufactured in the U.S.A.   SEPTEMBER 2, 2020

Scripture quotations are from New Revised Standard Version Bible, copyright © 1989 National Council of the Churches of Christ in the United States of America. Used by permission. All rights reserved worldwide.

Dedication

To the congregations I have served who opened their pulpits to me, especially: Reformation Lutheran Church in Media, PA, Spirit and Truth Worship Center in Yeadon, PA, United in Christ Lutheran Church in Lewisburg, PA, and St. Thomas Lutheran Church in Richmond, KY. I am grateful for your willingness to learn about and learn from apocalyptic texts and what they mean for our faith and our world. L. D. S.

To all the people who have been made afraid of God by misuses of apocalyptic texts and to those teachers and ministers who work to reclaim the message of joy and hope they contain. J. L. S.

Contents

Preface | xi

Chapter 1
An Introduction to Apocalyptic Thought | 1
—Jerry L. Sumney

Some Common Characteristics of Apocalyptic Writings | 2
The Origins of Apocalyptic Thought | 4
Some Important Aspects of Apocalyptic Thought | 7
The Early Church and Apocalyptic | 14
Conclusion | 15

Chapter 2
The Challenges—And Opportunities—of Apocalyptic Preaching | 16
—Leah D. Schade

Reflections on Christian Concepts of Time and Preaching | 18
"It's the end of the world as we know it and I feel_____"(fill in the blank) | 21
Not Our First Apocalyptic Rodeo | 23
Leaving Behind *Left Behind* | 26
Homiletical Orientation | 28

Chapter 3
Daniel 7:13, 15–18 | 32

An Exegesis of Daniel 7 | 32
—Jerry L. Sumney

Ideas for preaching | 39
—Leah D. Schade

Sermon: "Monsters and Saints: *Stranger Things* Meets Daniel 7" | 42
—Leah D. Schade

Chapter 4
Mark 13:24–37 (Year B—Advent—First Sunday in Advent) | 47

   An Exegesis of Mark 13 | 48
     —Jerry L. Sumney

   Ideas for Preaching Mark 13:24–37 | 56
     —Leah D. Schade

   Sermon: "Gathering Up the Fragments" | 59
     —Leah D. Schade

Chapter 5
Matthew 24:36–44 (Year A—Advent—First Sunday of Advent) | 64

   An Exegesis of Matthew 24:36–44 | 64
     —Jerry L. Sumney

   Ideas for Preaching on Matthew 24:36–44 | 69
     —Leah D. Schade

   Sermon: "Noah's Ark and Climate Change: What Kind of Church Will We Be?" | 72
     —Leah D. Schade

Chapter 6
Luke 21:25–36 (Year C—Advent—First Sunday in Advent) | 77

   An Exegesis of Luke 21:25–36 | 78
     —Jerry L. Sumney

   Ideas for Preaching on Luke 21:25–36 | 83
     —Leah D. Schade

   Sermon: "Gaining Our Souls" | 85
     —Leah D. Schade

Chapter 7
1 Corinthians 15:19–26 (Year C—Easter—Resurrection of the Lord) | 91

   An Exegesis of 1 Corinthians 15:19–26 | 91
     —Jerry L. Sumney

   Ideas for Preaching on 1 Corinthians 15:19–26 | 97
     —Leah D. Schade

   Sermon: "The Fleshy Faith of Resurrection: An Easter Sermon" | 100
     —Leah D. Schade

Chapter 8
1 Thessalonians 4:13–18 (Year A—Season after Pentecost —Proper 27 [32]) | 105

   An Exegesis of 1 Thessalonians 4:13–18 | 105
     —Jerry L. Sumney

   Ideas for preaching on 1 Thessalonians 4:13–18 | 111
     —Leah D. Schade

   Sermon: "The Pastoral Visit" | 114
     —Leah D. Schade

Chapter 9
1 Thessalonians 5:1–11 (Year A—Season after Pentecost —Proper 28 [33]) | 120

   An Exegesis of 1 Thessalonians 5:1–11 | 121
     —Jerry L. Sumney

   Sermon Ideas for 1 Thessalonians 5:1–11 | 126
     —Leah D. Schade

   Sermon: "Paying Attention to What Really Matters" | 128
     —Leah D. Schade

Chapter 10
Revelation 14:1–13 | 133

   Introduction to Revelation | 134
     —Jerry L. Sumney

   An Exegesis of Revelation 14 | 139
     —Jerry L. Sumney

   Ideas for Preaching on Revelation 14 | 144
     —Leah D. Schade

   Sermon: "Commemorating the Earth Martyrs" | 149
     —Leah D. Schade

Chapter 11
Revelation 21:1–6 (Year C—Easter—Fifth Sunday of Easter) | 153

   An Exegesis of Revelation 21:1–6 | 153
     —Jerry L. Sumney

   Ideas for Preaching on Revelation 21:1–6 | 157
     —Leah D. Schade

Sermon: "This World It IS My Home" | 161
—Leah D. Schade

Chapter 12
Revelation 21:10, 22—22:5 (Year C—Easter—Sixth Sunday of Easter) | 165

An Exegesis of Revelation 21:10, 22—22:5 | 166
—Jerry L. Sumney

Ideas for Preaching | 171
—Leah D. Schade

Sermon: "Shall We Gather at the River" | 175
—Leah D. Schade

Bibliography | 179

Preface

THIS BOOK IS INTENDED to help the church understand and proclaim the powerful messages that the Bible's apocalyptic texts contain. Preachers have often been reticent to preach on these texts because they seem too strange or they have been hijacked by people who use them in inappropriate ways. Besides, they also contain some material that seems threatening. But these texts have messages that can strengthen the church's resolve to be faithful, especially in ways that try to bring God's justice and love into the world. This may seem like an odd claim because it is sometimes (often) said that these texts encourage people to look only to heaven and a future end-time and so to ignore the things that violate God's will around them. This understanding of apocalyptic texts substantially misses what the texts want their readers to do. At their core, they want to encourage readers to live faithfully in this world.

This book is a joint effort of a homiletics scholar and a Bible scholar at Lexington Theological Seminary. The first chapter on understanding apocalyptic texts is written by Jerry L. Sumney, the Bible professor. Chapter two on preaching from apocalyptic texts is authored by Leah D. Schade, the homiletics professor. All of the following chapters are divided into three sections. The first section is an exegesis of the text by Sumney. The second and third parts are Ideas for Preaching and a sample sermon. Those two sections are written by Schade. However, we consulted with each other on our sections and worked together on the editing process.

Parts of this book are directly dependent on the early work, *Preaching Apocalyptic Texts* (St. Louis: Chalice, 1999), that was co-written by Sumney and Larry Paul Jones†, former homiletics professor at Lexington Theological Seminary. His premature passing took a powerful voice from the church. In that previous work, Dr. Jones wrote two sermons for each text for which Sumney wrote the exegesis. The discussion of apocalyptic

Preface

literature in chapter 1 of the present work is an expansion of a chapter in the previous work, and the exegesis of Daniel 7, Mark 13, and Revelation 14 are slight revisions of the exegesis in it. The exegesis work for 1 Thessalonians 4 and 5 in this work are notable expansions of the exegesis of those texts in the earlier book. None of Schade's Ideas for Sermons or her sermons depend on Dr. Jones's homiletical work in that earlier book. We are grateful to Michael Thomson and Cascade Press for seeing the importance of the message of these texts and being willing to include the parts of the book that were previously published.

The present book focuses most of its attention on texts from the Revised Common Lectionary. However, the chapter on Revelation 14 is included because of its oft-misunderstood and misinterpreted imagery and symbolism that has permeated both the church and the larger culture. We hope that this book will provide exegetical and homiletical guidance to enable ministers and others to preach from and teach about these texts. During these challenging and tumultuous times, we trust in God's power, mercy, and love to strengthen the church and renew hope for the world.

Leah D. Schade
Jerry L. Sumney

Chapter 1

An Introduction to Apocalyptic Thought

Jerry L. Sumney

How do you experience the world? Is it fair or unfair? Good or evil? Redeemable or beyond hope? You probably do not want to choose either alternative. Most people today find the truth somewhere in between these extremes. If that is the case for you, then apocalyptic writings will be somewhat foreign to your way of thinking. Though we do not often think about it, the theology each of us have has been influenced by our experience of the world. What we think about God, the world, and other humans (just to name a few things) is significantly affected by what has happened to us and how we interpret those events. If we are going to understand apocalyptic writings, we will need to know something about the ways the authors of such works think, so that we can begin to understand why they speak as they do about God, God's people, and God's enemies.

Apocalyptic writers usually view the world as completely captured by evil and as irredeemable without a catastrophic intervention of God. In their experience, there is something drastically wrong with the world. Apocalyptic writers are seeking a way to reconcile their belief in a good, powerful, and just God and their encounter with pervasive and successful evil.

In theological terms, one of the most basic issues apocalyptic thought wrestles with is theodicy: how does one explain injustice and evil in the world while holding to belief in a good and just God? This question is asked explicitly in several apocalyptic writings. In 2 Esdras,[1] the leading character looks about himself and sees the great sinfulness of the Babylonians who have conquered Israel. His question is, "Are the deeds of those who inhabit Babylon any better [than those of Israel]?" (2 Esdras 3:28). Then he complains that no one can understand what God has done and that God has given no explanation (see 3:28—4:36).

Apocalyptic arises in situations where the questions of theodicy become acute. The problem of evil in the world is always with us, but it becomes more important for an individual or a group when it is brought home, when you are the good person who is suffering unjustly. Groups adopt an apocalyptic outlook in times of crisis, when it seems they are being overwhelmed by their enemies, enemies who are beyond their capacity to defeat. Apocalyptic helps such groups interpret their experience in a way that preserves and strengthens their faith in God. Examples of such groups from the ancient world include the inhabitants of Qumran (who wrote the Dead Sea Scrolls), Jews living at the time of the Maccabean Revolt (see the discussion of the setting of Daniel in chapter 3 below), and Christians facing persecution. All of these groups faced overwhelming opposition or defeat while believing they were God's people. All asked, "How can God allow this? How will God respond to this?" Apocalyptic thought addresses these questions.

Apocalyptic responds by pointing beyond history, by asserting that the ultimate answer to these questions lies in another realm. So, it gives a larger context in which to understand the events of the world. It argues that earthly events are only one part of a cosmic drama that involves forces most people are unaware of, but which are now being revealed to God's people. It asserts that God will set things right in the end, that God's justice will be exercised. This satisfaction of God's justice includes both punishing the wicked and rewarding the group's faithfulness. On a personal level, it says that the last word is not said when you die; rather, there are rewards for the faithful individual.

SOME COMMON CHARACTERISTICS OF APOCALYPTIC WRITINGS

To understand the apocalyptic material in the Bible, it is useful to look at some common characteristics of apocalyptic writings. Through recognizing

---

1. This book is found in the Apocrypha.

An Introduction to Apocalyptic Thought

these characteristics, apocalyptic texts will be more accessible and more profitable as sources for Christian thought about and response to the world we know.

Apocalyptic writings are usually pseudepigraphic, i.e., written by someone other than the person by whom the document claims to be written.[2] While this sounds like plagiarism to us, it was a widespread practice in the ancient world. Writers were castigated if they were caught writing in the name of another person, but many thought it was worth the risk because the message they wanted to get across was so important. We find, for example, works that were written in the name of Socrates more than 300 years after he died. Writers often used this technique when they thought they represented the thought of the claimed writer and so could bring the earlier person's insight to bear on the actual writer's situation. Jewish and Christian apocalyptic writings often claim to be written by someone known from the Bible who lived long before the actual writing (e.g., Enoch, Ezra, Baruch, Abraham, etc.).

Apocalyptic writings claim that they contain a revelation from God that consists of knowledge that has been hidden from all but a very few people but is now revealed to the wider circle of the people of God because the end is near. They often contain information about angels, the ordering of the cosmos, or the nature of heavenly realms. This knowledge is usually given to the writer by an angelic mediator. The writer's claim to authority comes primarily from the assertion that what is written is directly a revelation from God.

Connected with their pseudonymity, apocalyptic writings often include *ex eventu* prophecy. This means that they have their supposed writer predict something that is in the future for that figure but is a past event for the real author. When Enoch, who is taken from Genesis 5, has correctly predicted the history of the world from the Flood to the second century BCE (when it was actually written), the reader has good reason to think he will also be right about what is to come next. So *ex eventu* prophecy gives assurance to the reader that what the writer says is trustworthy. This sure word is precisely what those who are suffering need.

Finally, the most basic point apocalyptic writers want to establish is that God will make things right. All apocalyptic thought asserts that God

---

2. Revelation is an exception. It seems to have been written by the person named in the greeting, John, a Jewish church member who addressed the churches and was revered as a prophet.

will be true to God's own nature by defeating evil and establishing justice for the faithful. God will establish a reign of justice and goodness which evil cannot overcome. The readers can take courage, even in the most dire circumstances, that this is the certain end and that they will be included in this victory of God. All the other characteristics of apocalyptic are intended to help establish this point.

Not all apocalyptic texts have all of these characteristics (e.g., Revelation has no *ex eventu* prophecy), but they give us a place to start as we investigate this material.

THE ORIGINS OF APOCALYPTIC THOUGHT

Our understanding of apocalyptic thought will also be enhanced if we know something about the origins of this type of thought. Two related questions bear on this issue: When did apocalyptic thought emerge? and What are its sources? We begin with the second question. There have been many suggestions about where the roots of apocalyptic thought are to be found. Some have argued that it only drew on Hebrew prophetic thought, others that it was derived solely from Wisdom traditions, and still others that the strongest influences came from Persian or Greek thought. Most interpreters think apocalyptic thought drew on all of these resources when facing certain types of social circumstances.

Most interpreters also agree that the primary source for apocalyptic is Hebrew prophecy. The faith of the Hebrew prophets always had an eschatological orientation. They believed in a God who worked in the world and who would bring about God's own purposes, including establishing the triumphant rule of God. The prophets never doubted that God's purposes would win out in the end. Apocalyptic thought refocuses this belief, giving more emphasis to the final conclusion. Given that the return from exile did not begin a period of national prominence in which God was clearly ruler of the world, and given the failure of other nationalistic hopes expressed by the prophets, apocalyptic thought relocated those hopes outside the realm of history. They began to look for their fulfillment in a more dramatic movement by God, an action which affected history but was brought in from another realm.

In addition to this stream of thought from the prophets, apocalyptic drew on characteristics often found in the Wisdom tradition. Daniel is an interpreter of dreams, a function usually associated with the Wisdom tradition rather than prophets. Daniel, the leading character in the apocalyptic book which bears his name, is even ranked among the "wise men" in Babylonia (Dan 4:68). Additionally, some of the determinism found in Wisdom thought was appropriated as apocalyptic thought developed. Apocalypticists are certain about the outcome of history and the main lines of the course of history. This is seen not only in its confidence that God's reign will be established, but also in the foretelling of world history found in many apocalyptic texts. This certainty about the course of history and its ultimate outcome does not necessarily mean that human free will is diminished. In apocalyptic thought humans are free to make their own choices about whether they will be on God's side or that of evil. So some events of history are determined, but it is up to the individual to respond to God appropriately. The importance of free will can also be seen in the apocalyptic writers' belief that individuals will be judged by God.

The prophetic and wisdom traditions cannot, however, account for all one finds in apocalyptic. It seems clear that its dualism, its development of traditions about angels, and its cosmology are significantly influenced by Greek and Persian thought. Thus, many sources contributed to the kind of thought which is found in apocalyptic writings. Materials from these various traditions were combined and synthesized to create a way of thinking, a way of perceiving God, the world, and themselves that made sense of the addressed communities' experience.

What finally brings all these influences together into what we recognize as apocalyptic thought are the circumstances of life faced by particular communities. While no one type of situation can be said to produce apocalyptic, it may be broadly characterized as crisis literature. It developed when communities were under great stress, stress that threatened their belief in the power, goodness, and justice of God. Sometimes this was a national crisis, other times it was simply a crisis for the group. The best terms to describe the situations in which apocalyptic thought did (and does) develop are relative deprivation and cognitive dissonance. In a situation that involves relative deprivation, the group is deprived of some status, position, authority, or other value that they believe they should have but do not, in fact, possess. So a comparatively well-off group could develop an apocalyptic mind-set if they were convinced they were being deprived of something of significant value because of their religious beliefs. This experience of opposition from those outside the group can arise from circumstances that are not historically significant but nevertheless have a great impact on the group affected. It is the experience of oppression that is important for the development of apocalyptic thought, not the historical significance of what causes the group to feel this way.

The term *cognitive dissonance* may also be appropriately applied to many such situations. This expression describes a situation in which there is significant disparity between what one thinks and what one experiences. Again, this does not have to be a circumstance that has a noticeable effect on world or even local history; it simply involves a perceived great difference between what one expects and thinks ought to be and what is felt to be the reality. In our cases, those who believe they are God's people expect this identity to enhance their status but just the opposite seems to be happening. For the early church, becoming a member of the movement meant a person had begun to worship the only true God. Members gave up participation in other cults to be associated with this God. But instead of this leading to blessings and good fortune, it led to disadvantage and persecution. Such experiences could be interpreted as evidence that they had made the wrong choice. Apocalyptic thought tries to reconcile who the people of God know themselves to be and what they think that identity means with the ways they perceive their existence at that moment in time.

Whether seen more as cognitive dissonance or relative deprivation, apocalyptic develops in situations in which a group feels deprived and sees the world to be in a crisis. Things are not what they should be or, more importantly, what God wants them to be. Since the group is powerless to change the situation, the only solution is an act of God, an act in which God destroys the current world order and establishes an order in which justice and goodness are dominant.

The type of situation described here as that which provides fertile ground for the seeds of apocalyptic to grow was present in the second century BCE in Palestine. As the discussion of the historical context of Daniel in chapter three will show, this was a period in which people were persecuted and killed precisely because they were remaining faithful to God. This seems to be the moment when the various elements of the mix came together to form what we know as apocalyptic. It is at this point that belief in judgment after death and in the resurrection of the righteous take hold within Judaism. By this moment in history the Jews have had extensive exposure to Persian and Greek ideas and they have had to begin to reinterpret the messages of the prophets because their hopes for national prominence had not materialized. Thus, apocalyptic thought comes to prominence in the desperate struggle in Judea, probably between 200 and 150 BCE.

SOME IMPORTANT ASPECTS OF APOCALYPTIC THOUGHT

It will help us understand apocalyptic texts if we know something about how most apocalyptic writers think about God, the nature of humanity, and ethics. These are among some of the most important issues that these writings address.

The nature of God in apocalyptic thought

The topic of the nature of God is not a common one in apocalyptic writings, but some characteristics of God stand out as very important for this way of thinking. This topic is also important because maintaining belief in God is one of the primary functions of apocalyptic thought. As a means to help us understand apocalyptic, we will focus our attention on three other matters: God's transcendence, sovereignty, and justice.

All apocalyptic writers agree that God is personal, powerful, and holy, but there is a debate among scholars over whether apocalyptic thought reflects a view of God that sees God as increasingly transcendent and so less immanent. Some scholars see the rise of a developed angelology (the study of angels and ranks of angels) as a sign that God is no longer as accessible as God had been when the prophets spoke of God as a parent. In some apocalyptic writings, angels seem to be the link between God and the world; occasionally angels even appear as mediators between God and people who pray.

However, in some of these same writings (e.g., 1 Enoch[3]) we find immediate acts of God performed with no mediation. Additionally, in books like Daniel the characters obviously have direct access to God in prayer and God acts directly throughout the stories. Other apocalyptic writings also teach that God acts directly among humans (e.g., 2 Esdras). What we find, then, is that apocalyptic works do not all agree on this matter, but those who think God is accessible only through intermediaries are a distinct minority. Furthermore, a developed angelology does not necessarily

---

3. This writing is found in the Pseudepigrapha.

mean that God is thought to be distant. The War Scroll from Qumran has an extensively developed angelology, but it also has God "in our midst" in the final battle. What all of these apocalyptic writers do agree on is that God must be separated from the evil in the world. All of them see God's holiness as inviolable. Thus, while God may be in direct contact with the world, God does not come into contact with evil.

Belief in the sovereignty of God is essential for apocalyptic. One of the main points of apocalyptic writings is to assure the readers that, in spite of evidence to the contrary, God is sovereign. We see this in the confidence these writers have that the plan of God is moving forward. It is further demonstrated in the extensive *ex eventu* prophecy found in some apocalyptic writings. These elements of apocalyptic discourse are evidence for a historical determinism. They show that these writers believe that history, at least its main outline and final outcome, has been ordained and arranged by God. The certainty of God's final victory is central to apocalyptic thought. This theme stands out especially clearly in Daniel. In the story in which Nebuchadnezzar becomes like an animal, Daniel declares to the king three times (4:17, 25, 26) that God is sovereign, and the story ends with Nebuchadnezzar acknowledging this very point (4:34). God's sovereignty is also a theme which runs through all the visions of Daniel 7.

This point is so important in apocalyptic writings because the writers and the readers seem to be living in a world that is ruled by evil, a world in which God is not sovereign. In fact, most apocalyptic thinkers are convinced that the world is not currently ruled by God. This is certainly the viewpoint of the New Testament writers. Though most Christians today are used to thinking that God is in control of our lives and our world, apocalypticists were (and are) convinced that this was not the case. They emphasize that the current domination of the world by evil is temporary. They assert that even though the world is presently ruled by the forces of evil, the true sovereign of the entire cosmos will soon act. The God who is the ultimate King will reclaim what rightfully belongs to God and will punish the usurpers along with their accomplices and will reward those who have been faithful to God. Without such a belief in the sovereignty of God, apocalyptic faith—indeed any Christian faith—cannot exist.

Apocalypticists are also convinced that God is just. Belief in the justice of God is another primary motivation for apocalyptic thought. That the world is ruled by evil and that the righteous are those who suffer most are only problems if one believes God is just. So apocalyptic seeks ways to show that God's justice will be exercised and will be the final word. This belief is manifested in the development of the ideas of judgment after death and of the resurrection.

Judgment is a central characteristic of apocalyptic thought. At the heart of all apocalyptic speculation about judgment is the conviction that God will not let God's people be destroyed by their enemies. Judgment is necessarily related to their belief in the justice of God, because for justice to reign, evil must be punished and good must be rewarded (see 1 Enoch 102:1; 103:18). This is a logically necessary element of belief in a just (i.e., fair) God. So in the face of persecution, the ethical faiths of Judaism and Christianity opted for the belief that God's righteousness is exercised in a realm beyond earthly life. Judgment in apocalyptic is usually based on morality. In Judaism this meant faithfulness to the Law; in Christianity it meant adhering to Christian morality as understood in a particular community and not denying the faith in persecution.

It was also this belief in the justice of God which led to the belief in the resurrection of the dead within Judaism. The idea of an afterlife which offered more than fading away in Sheol had been growing within Judaism since about the fifth century BCE, but it was the events associated with the Maccabean Revolt (see below the introduction to Daniel) that finally resulted in a fairly widespread belief in the resurrection of at least some of the dead. Just before and during the time of this revolt, Jews were executed precisely for being faithful to God and the Torah (see the graphic story of the torture and execution of seven brothers and their mother in 4 Maccabees[4]). Such terrible events, of course, push the question of the justice of God to the forefront. How can God be just and allow people to be tortured to death for their faith? Since God did not rescue these martyrs as God rescued the faithful in the stories of Daniel, there must be some other way in which the justice of God is satisfied.

God's justice demands that the righteousness and faithfulness of these martyrs be rewarded. Because of this divine necessity, belief in an afterlife for the righteous flowered in this period. At the beginning, only the extraordinarily righteous or martyrs and the extraordinarily wicked had an afterlife, but as time passed most Jews came to believe that all persons participated in the afterlife.[5] So belief in a resurrection that included judgment

---

4. This writing is found in the Apocrypha.

5. The Sadducees are the exception to this trend. They seem not to have believed in an afterlife for anyone. They were also among those who did not adopt an apocalyptic

grew out of the injustices experienced by communities that held firmly to their belief in a sovereign and just God.

We should not think, however, that judgment based on morality requires that apocalypticists be legalists. That is far from the case. Only a very few apocalyptic writings (e.g., 3 Baruch[6]) assert that judgment is based solely on one's deserts. Most acknowledge that people are found righteous in judgment only through God's grace and mercy. God's grace does not impede the exercise of God's justice; they are necessarily cooperative but each equally necessary. Again, judgment based on morality does not mean judgment without grace and it does not mean legalism. You can see this in the Qumran War Scroll (ch. 11) when it says that God delivers God's people through God's loving kindness and not according to their works. Similarly, 2 Esdras trusts that since humans cannot overcome their evil tendency, God will supply grace at judgment. When apocalypticists think of judgment, fear is not their first thought. Rather, this is the moment when retribution is meted out to their and God's enemies. They certainly do not lose sight of the accountability judgment brings to them, but they trust God to fulfill God's purposes and nature by bringing them into the place God has prepared for God's people.

The idea of God being just in judgment makes modern people nervous. We are more ready to focus our attention on God's love and mercy, thinking that these are the opposite of justice. But they are not. If God is not just, then God is unjust. The alternative to God being just is that God is unfair, that God plays favorites or is capricious. This unhappy alternative would mean we could never trust God. Furthermore, the justice of God is the basis for all Christian calls for justice in the world. Since Christian ethics is based on the character of God, we have no basis for working for justice, including equal rights for all people, unless we believe in the unshakable justice of God. So apocalyptic brings us back to a characteristic of God with which we are less than comfortable, but which is essential to who God is and to what makes God a God we can trust and a God who is worthy of worship.

---

outlook.

6 This is another work found in the Pseudepigrapha.

Human nature in apocalyptic thought

To understand the view of human nature seen in our material we must begin with a survey of how human nature was seen in the Hebrew Bible. Instead of finding one consistent view of human nature in the Hebrew Scriptures, there is a development in thought within Israel about this matter. In the traditions found in the Pentateuch, the individual was not as important as the group. One's family or tribe always took precedence over the individual. This emphasis on the group meant that the way one lived on after death was through what she or he had contributed to the well-being of the group. Thus, the afterlife for individuals was envisioned only to a very limited extent. When people died they went to Sheol, at least temporarily. This was not a pleasant place; it was a place where one is powerless, where one cannot even remember the goodness of Yahweh. There were no moral distinctions in Sheol and eventually you fade out of existence.

The prophets begin to give more place to the individual. The emphasis is still on the group and the reward of the righteous is primarily the good of Israel and of one's descendants, but some ideas about the continuance of the individual emerge. The importance of the individual emerges especially clearly in Jeremiah and Ezekiel. In Ezekiel 18, the result of a person's sin is to be visited on them alone rather than on their children (or by extension their nation). This separation of the fate of the individual from that of the group is a somewhat different perspective from what we see in the Pentateuch and is the sort of thought that prepares the way for the views we find in apocalyptic.

All apocalypticists believe that humans continue to exist after death. As we have already seen, the experiences of persecution and martyrdom seemed to require some avenue other than what happens in this world for the expression of God's righteousness and justice. Clearly martyrs were not dealt with justly in this world. Outside the thought of apocalyptic, martyrs were sometimes seen as receiving the punishment due to the nation and thus paving the way for Israel's restoration. But the continuing unfaithfulness of some in Israel seemed to make national restoration impossible. So personal rewards and punishments become the ways God responds to faithfulness and wickedness. Beyond this concern about justice, the desire for continued fellowship with God and with the fellow faithful pushed forward the belief in an afterlife with rewards and punishments. This belief could also be seen as a type of fulfillment of national hopes since the individual was not blessed in isolation, but with others who were faithful.

With the exception of a very few documents (most notably Jubilees[7]), apocalyptic writers (including the Apostle Paul) envisioned the afterlife as a resurrection of the body, not as the immortality of the soul. The idea of a resurrection of the body is consistent with the Hebrew idea that a human is a unitary psycho-physical unit. That is, they did not separate the body and soul, giving the soul a higher value, as the Greeks had done. Thus, a person cannot be complete or happy without both body and soul. Sheol had been a place where one had no body and such existence could only be temporary and could not be considered true life. So apocalyptic continues to see human personality as a unity rather than as a duality. Believing in the resurrection of the body did not mean that life was always conceived of as bound to material, earthy existence. Rather, they sometimes looked forward to the transformation of the body, a transformation which suited the body for life with God. A fairly extended explication of this notion is found in chapter 7 on 1 Corinthians 15.

Ethics in apocalyptic thought

In this section we turn our attention to what humans are held accountable for in apocalyptic thought. Only a very few scholars whose major field of research is apocalyptic have argued that apocalyptic has no concern for ethics because it has separated the kingdom of God from earthly realities. As this view has it, apocalyptic, rather than being socially responsible, becomes preoccupied with the damnation of the oppressor or with blessings in another realm. Though this is a common perception about apocalyptic thought among non-specialists, most scholars reject this interpretation and many assert that ethics is central to apocalyptic.

The expectation of judgment found in all apocalyptic implies that ethics is central even when it is not explicitly discussed. One of the primary reasons authors wrote apocalyptic texts was to encourage faithfulness to God and loyalty to the Law of God, even if it leads one to death. All apocalyptic is hortatory. Discourses that encourage ethical living and specify what that means are common in apocalyptic texts. Encouraging faithful (i.e., ethical) living was a primary goal of Daniel 1–6 and in 2 Esdras the sole characteristic of the saved is holiness. Another indicator of the importance of ethics in this way of thinking is the way life in the messianic future is described: it is in accordance with God's Law.

7. This writing is also part of the Pseudepigrapha.

An Introduction to Apocalyptic Thought

In Jewish apocalypses the Law was the ethical ideal both now and in the age to come. The authors of these texts saw no antagonism between being required to keep the Law and eschatological confidence. As they saw them, both the Law and apocalyptic actions by God were expressions of God's covenant with them and so were blessings.

Given the emphasis on judgment found in apocalyptic thought, it is not surprising that individual accountability is important. People are accountable before God for their transgressions of God's Law and will. The unfaithful are accountable because they have refused the ways of God. Thus, the distinctions among those who have died are based on their conduct while on earth. Again, this does not mean apocalypticists were legalists; rather, most of them recognized that the only way anyone could stand before God was if God exercised mercy.

Some interpreters argue that the apocalyptic outlook leads to a passive ethic, an ethic that encourages people simply to submit to persecution. Some apocalyptic works (e.g., the Assumption of Moses[8]) do recommend quietism, but this seems to be against the general trend. The Jewish uprisings throughout the Roman period show that apocalyptic is often not passive because these revolts were often tied to apocalyptic hopes. Most of these many rebellions, and there were many, expected God to intervene to overthrow the Romans. At the same time, God would establish those who instigated the uprising, who identified themselves as God's people, in positions of power. The War Scroll of Qumran offers us a specific example of this way of thinking. Its author expects the community to be active participants in the end time battle. Thus, many apocalyptic groups clearly thought they had an active role to play in God's plan.

Though some have asserted that apocalyptic's attention to the future world leads people not to be concerned about present conditions in this world, that is not necessarily the case. The Damascus Document, written for lay people who were associated with the Qumran community and so with an apocalyptic worldview, has a clear concern for social justice (see esp. ch. 1). Second Enoch also encourages social justice through its attention to issues involving money, the courts, and the poor. So apocalyptic does not entirely abandon the world to evil. The people of God are expected to act justly and to work for a more just world, even though the forces against them are overwhelming.

---

8. Yet another writing among the Pseudepigrapha.

Apocalypse When?

THE EARLY CHURCH AND APOCALYPTIC

All of the authors of the books of the New Testament had an apocalyptic worldview. While they do not all write in the genre of apocalyptic texts, they all write from that perspective. The book of Revelation is the only New Testament book written fully in the style of apocalyptic, but other books have sections that adopt that style. We deal with some of them in this book.

Yet, there was a difference between the apocalyptic outlook of church members and other apocalyptic thinkers. The church was built on belief in the resurrection of Christ. The resurrection of Christ vindicated Jesus' ministry and message, but it did much more. Apocalyptic writers see the resurrection of the dead as an event of the end. It is a sign that the end has come. The earliest church understood the resurrection of Christ as the beginning of the general resurrection of the dead. It meant that the last days were upon them. The earliest believers in Christ expected that general resurrection to come very soon. Of course, it did not.

As the church thought about the delay in the coming of the end, it also experienced the presence of God in new ways. Among the most notable was the giving of the Spirit. Acts 2 has Peter interpret the coming of the Spirit at Pentecost as a gift of the last days (2:17–21). It was clear that the fullness of the end had not come, that evil had not been defeated; the Romans were still in charge and they were still being persecuted for their faith. But still, they experienced a part—a foretaste—of that final victory of God through this experience of the Spirit. It was not the fullness of being in the very presence of God with all troubles overcome, but it was a new act of God in the world. This new presence of God is a sign that the end has begun. All of the time of the church is the end times because it comes after the resurrection of Christ that inaugurated the coming of God's kingdom with its defeat of evil.

There is a sense, then, in which the church possesses gifts of the end, and a sense in which it does not. There is an "already" aspect of the church's experience of the final state of all things (the presence of the Spirit in our lives), and a "not yet" aspect (we do not yet possess all God will give at the end). The idea that we possess an "already" part of the end-times blessings is often called a partially realized eschatology. If we believed that we possessed all of God's gifts now, we would have a fully realized eschatology. New Testament writers regularly reject versions of a fully realized eschatology. They keep that tension between experiencing a beginning of blessings of the end and looking forward to the final consummation of God's intentions for the world.

Our book is written with a partially realized eschatological outlook. With the New Testament writers, we think that the resurrection of Christ opened a new kind of presence of God in the world. In this time the Spirit strengthens the people of God to work for what God wants for the world. But we also hold the hope for a future act of God that will make all things conform to God's will and character.

CONCLUSION

Hopefully, this brief introduction to apocalyptic thought will prepare the reader to understand better the texts we treat in the following parts of this book. The writings we will look at come from a variety of genres, yet they all participate in the thought world described here. These writings are all seeking ways to make sense of their belief in a good, powerful, and just God given their experience of the world as a place ruled by evil. They do this in large part by asserting that God will act soon in ways that decisively vindicate God's nature as they understand it. At the same time, they also want to encourage their readers to remain faithful to God in very difficult circumstances.

Chapter 2

The Challenges—And Opportunities—of Apocalyptic Preaching

Leah D. Schade

For clergy, preaching apocalyptic texts is anticipated with nearly as much enthusiasm as a dental check-up. "The end of the world . . . again," quipped one pastor at a text study I once attended as we tackled the images of the end times that proliferate the Revised Common Lectionary passages in the last Sundays of Pentecost and the first Sundays of Advent. The pastor's sarcasm perhaps masks a deeper unease about the real fears alluded to in passages such as Revelation 21:15, whose warnings of impending cosmic upheaval ricochet sharply off contemporary headlines about war, natural disasters, and threats to the fabric of civilization. Add to this the disconcerting news about the effects of climate disruption, a global pandemic, and environmental stress, and the task of preaching good news in the face of seemingly imminent doom can feel overwhelming to pastor and congregation alike.

Catherine Keller describes the problem this way:

> [W]arnings of social, economic, ecological, or nuclear disaster have become so numbingly normal that they do not have the desired effect on most of us who retreat all the more frantically into private pursuits . . . How can we sustain resistance to destruction without expecting to triumph? That is, how can we acknowledge the apocalyptic dimensions of the late-modern situation in which we find ourselves entrenched without either clinging to some

The Challenges—And Opportunities—of Apocalyptic Preaching

millennial hope of steady progress or then, flipping, disappointed, back to pessimism?[1]

Preachers may experience this "flipping" when faced with the temptations of either cheerleading the faithful with end-time fantasies or encouraging magical thinking by waiting passively for a messianic solution to the world's problems. Both options, says Keller, can lead to an "apocalyptic either/or logic—if we can't save the world, then to hell with it. Either salvation or damnation."[2]

This either-or dichotomy is not the only option to approaching end-time texts, however. New Testament scholar Barbara Rossing notes that apocalyptic texts provide unique opportunities for preachers and are, in fact, essential because they "empower radical witness. They give us a sacramental imagination, taking us on a journey into the heart of God's vision for the world."[3] The word *apokalypsis* in Greek literally means, "pulling back the curtain." Biblical texts (and the sermons that utilize them) can pull back the veils that obscure the presence of systemic and oppressive evil in the world and allow us to see a deeper reality that is not immediately visible. We are able to see with a kind of double vision that reveals "both the beauty of creation and also the pathologies of empire," whether these empires originate in Assyria, Babylonia, Rome, or the United States of America.[4]

Equipped with this double vision, the preacher is able to name the underlying oppressive assumptions of empire and critique these assumptions and how they manifest in society, the natural world, and the lived experiences of the hearers. But a third move is needed—proclaiming the divine eschatological vision that has the power to transform our imaginations, renew hope, and empower collective action for living into this vision of the eschaton. *Eschatology* comes from the Greek word *eschaton*, meaning end times. The visionary world of biblical apocalyptic literature "can help us see both the perils we face and the urgency of God's promised future," says Rossing, "turning the world for justice and healing, 'on Earth as in heaven.' The preacher cultivates an apocalyptic imagination by helping people recognize God's future breaking into the present, even in times of despair."[5]

1. Keller, *Apocalypse Now and Then*, 14.
2. Keller, *Apocalypse Now and Then*, 14.
3. Rossing, "The World is About to Turn," 141.
4. Rossing, "The World is About to Turn," 141.
5. Rossing, "The World is About to Turn," 141.

Our approach to preaching apocalyptic texts in this book will be to offer an eschatological perspective that is forthright about the existential realities of our present time while avoiding either extreme of doom and gloom or "pie in the sky by and by." We'll explore a "third way" for understanding the concepts of beginnings and endings in Scripture that looks to the hope revealed in Christ's redemption for all Creation.[6] The goal is for this lens to yield insights and heuristic possibilities for eschatologically oriented proclamation that engenders hope and invites deep and joyful engagement with God's new creation.

REFLECTIONS ON CHRISTIAN CONCEPTS OF TIME AND PREACHING

The way in which the church has understood time throughout its history, how it orients itself in time today, and how its worship rituals, Bible readings, prayers, and even music are shaped by the liturgical year are all factors to consider in preaching, especially when addressing apocalyptic texts. Genesis 1 describes the creation of time where days and nights are marked by the movement of the sun and moon and stars, the means by which Earth-dwellers measure and track time. By the end of that chapter, we reach the culmination of the seven-day period resolving into a time of rest. Thus, we see patterns: the movement of light and darkness within a single day, the seven-day week within the month, and all of this encompassed within the cycle of the year. Thus, our very existence contains the DNA of time built right into the cosmos, our planet, our bodies and psyches, and our communities.

Yet humans also have a sense of the eternal, the timelessness of the Divine. Psalm 90 gives us a glimpse into the mystery of how mortals and God experience time differently:

> [1]LORD, you have been our dwelling place in all generations.
> [2]Before the mountains were brought forth, or ever you had formed the earth and the world, from everlasting to everlasting you are God.

---

6. I make the decision to capitalize the word *Creation* so as to denote the level of respect I am affording the other-than-human world as a *subject* rather than object. I do the same with the term *Earth* when addressing it as an entity (as opposed to lowercase *earth*, which is a synonym of *soil*). Capitalizing the term indicates that this is an entity with a name, and that the entity is worthy of such.

The Challenges—And Opportunities—of Apocalyptic Preaching

> ³You turn us back to dust, and say, "Turn back, you mortals."
> ⁴For a thousand years in your sight are like yesterday when it is past, or like a watch in the night. With the LORD one day is like a thousand years, and a thousand years are like one day.

In other words, what can seem like a long span of time for humans is but a tick of the clock for God. Perceptions of time differ according to our perspective; time stretches, contracts, speeds up, slows down, and even seems to stop on occasion. More importantly, as Jews and Christians believe, God chooses mortal time as the means by which to reveal God's self. Humans are not expected to train themselves to transcend time and space in order to attain enlightenment, as is the case in some religions. Instead, God enters into human time and space in very concrete ways, through specific historical events and people, in order to develop a relationship with humankind. Relationships are key for human beings, and we both mark time and build continuity in relationships by remembering certain days such as birthdays and anniversaries throughout the years. The same is true for Jews and Christians who believe in a relational God who makes Godself known through concrete acts that happen in history and are remembered yearly, weekly, and even daily.

In this way, time—past, present, and future—is a gift that is given to humanity. The fact that God is interested in being part of time with us and for us creates *sacred time* for believers. Mircea Eliade theorized that Archaic Man lived in the space between two planes of existence—the sacred and the profane. Human belief in the supernatural means that their actions, rituals, buildings, and how they orient themselves in time are all reflected by the desire to exist in the sacred realm even while slogging through the everydayness of life. Profane time is experienced as linear. It's just one thing happening after another in sequence. Time flows in one direction, from present to future. But human memory also allows for time past to be remembered in the present, thus seeming to flow both backward and forward. We have the capacity to remember not only as individuals, but also as a species, as a culture. This past is remembered through story, myth, and recorded history. We also have the capacity to think about the future, to conceive of a different reality than what we see at the present. This future-thinking accounts for the tension in apocalyptic—will the future be an improvement on the past, or will we see things deteriorate? And what is God's role in this future? What is the church's role? What is the role of individual Christians?

Apocalypse When?

In addition to the linear conceptions of time, humans are also able to experience time in a cyclical way, which is how we are able to imagine and exist in sacred time. We do this through ritual in which we attempt to re-create and thus re-experience the events of the past through sacred time. This cyclical nature of time enables us to re-actualize what happened previously, even going back to the dawn of human civilization. For example, seasons of planting, growth, harvest, and death are marked in nearly every ancient culture, including the Jewish calendar (which is, of course, where the Christian calendar draws its origins). But these seasons are also given sacred significance, connected with the realm of God as well as the stories of God's saving history with the people.

Human culture celebrates all manner of festivals around the change of seasons and years, and this is no different in the church. The liturgical year marks both the internal cycles of time (Advent, Christmas, Epiphany, Lent, Easter, Pentecost), and the progression of time over weeks, months, years, centuries, and millennia. Eliade explained that through myths and rituals that give access to this sacred time, humans can protect themselves against what he called the "terror of history," the fear that human existence is a pointless exercise ending in oblivion.[7] In other words, sacred time always involves a return to a paradigmatic mythic period in the past in order to give meaning to the present and to bolster courage for the future.

For Christians, the liturgy within our worship services gives us access to that sacred time. Both the cyclical and linear timelines converge because God is active in history, is active in the here and now, and will be active in the future—what the Greeks called *eschaton*, the end times. Every worship service in a sense proclaims the in-breaking of God's kingdom into this world, bringing the fullness of time upon us. This means that the liturgy (and thus preaching) situates us in that liminal, in-between time which transcends past, present, and future, but is also very much a part of real time as well.

How does God's future manifest itself in our present time? There is another interesting Greek word called *prolepsis*, which means "anticipated." When we participate in and lead the liturgy, we are in the midst of a paradox: Christ's coming has already happened, but it has not yet come upon us in the fullness of the present moment. We can catch glimpses of it, but we only experience his return (called the Parousia) in an "already but not yet" way. Thus, we exist in a state of anticipation and expectation. Prolepsis

---

7. Eliade, *The Myth of the Eternal Return*, ch. 4.

allows the liturgy (including the sermon) to create hope because it anticipates the return of the resurrected Christ within this very time and place.

Think of it this way. Ephesians 1:9–10, states: "[God] has made known to us the mystery of his will, according to his good pleasure that he set forth in Christ, as a plan for the fullness of time, to gather up all things in him, things in heaven and things on earth." In other words, time is moving forward to an inexorable point of Christ's coming, the fulfillment of the kingdom of God at the eschaton. And because we believe that promise, it has an effect on the here and now, so that in our proclamation, in our worship, in our service, in our work for justice and peace, we are actually participating in the coming of God's realm. We are part of Christ's work of bringing the realm of God into the world—even when it seems the world is falling apart around us.

Thus, it is through Jesus the Christ that past, present, and future come together. And we experience that mysterious convergence through the rituals of the liturgy where we read from ancient Scriptures, preach, and partake in ancient rituals (such as baptism and communion) that have been with us for thousands of years. As Hebrews 1:12 states: "Long ago God spoke to our ancestors in many and various ways by the prophets, but in these last days he has spoken to us by a Son, whom he appointed heir of all things, through whom he also created the worlds." The question for preachers and their listeners, however, is how to live in these "last days" when suffering seems to be increasing on scales of magnitude that are overwhelming.

"IT'S THE END OF THE WORLD AS WE KNOW IT AND I FEEL _____"(FILL IN THE BLANK)[8]

"We are moving fast—nose-diving—toward ecological catastrophe and/or nuclear Armageddon. If we cannot pull out of this nose-dive the short term future can evaporate at any moment."[9] So warned feminist psychologist Dorothy Dinnerstein in 1989. She continued: "And to pull out of it—to avert the death of living earthly reality—means mustering a huge, miraculous spurt of human growth and change: fast change; change within persons and within intimate groups, and change in the nature of the larger

---

8. The song "It's the End of the World as We Know It (And I Feel Fine)" is a song by the band R.E.M. released on their 1987 album *Document*.

9. Dinnerstein, "Survival on Earth," 192.

societal units (cultural, economic, political and regional) on whose level the developments we call historic take place."[10]

Voices within the secular realm have joined in the clarion call for action in the face of impending apocalyptic doom. Thomas Friedman's book, *Hot, Flat and Crowded: Why We Need a Green Revolution—and How it can Renew America*, attempted to tap into the can-do spirit of American ingenuity to avert the disastrous trifecta of global warming, the demands of the global economy, and human overpopulation.[11] Al Gore's *Earth in the Balance: Ecology and the Human Spirit* called for a "global Marshall Plan" to respond to the global environmental crisis and even evoked religious language. "We have had a warning of the fate that awaits if we 'bow before the accomplished fact.' God and history will remember our judgment," he solemnly intoned.[12] Nearly thirty years later at the time of this writing, climate scientists have estimated that the time remaining is terrifyingly short for humans to radically curtail carbon emissions before a cascade of catastrophic events threatens all life on this planet.

In many ways Creation itself is already *in* the eschaton. This is especially true for the strip-mined mountains, decimated forests, and other devastated areas of Earth for whom "the end" has already happened. The preacher working from an eco-hermeneutical reading of Revelation might consider Earth and Earth's other-than-human creatures as "hearers" of the sermon even if they are not present per se in the human congregation. Because, in fact, the "end of the world" has already come to pass for countless extinct species whose history has come to an end at the hands of human beings. Doomsday has come and gone for the North American Passenger Pigeon, Australian Toolache Wallaby, Indian Arunchal Hopea Tree, and St. Helena Olive, not to mention untold numbers of plant and animal species whose final dying members passed into oblivion unnoticed and unmourned by human eyes.

And what of the impending apocalypse for the hundreds of plant and animal species currently facing threatened or imminent extinction? Countless species languish in prisons of shrinking habitat, poisoned waters, and diminishing food supplies. We have ghettoized Creation, delineating by way of concrete and metal boundaries where greenery, fur, and feathers can and cannot live, blocking them into increasingly smaller areas of living

10. Dinnerstein, "Survival on Earth," 192.
11. Friedman, *Hot, Flat, and Crowded*.
12. Gore, *Earth in the Balance*, 294.

The Challenges—And Opportunities—of Apocalyptic Preaching

that isolate and cramp them in what had once been vast and free-ranging bioscapes. Meanwhile, human suffering from the effects of climate disruption manifests in catastrophic storms, rising sea levels engulfing homes, droughts and blighted crops, wildfires raging through entire communities, and wars over diminishing resources.

This means that when we read John of Patmos's vision of the Four Horsemen of the Apocalypse in Revelation, we can see that this is not some otherworldly portent of impending doom. They represent real human riders subjugating animals, ecosystems, and humans (especially those of color and those in poverty) in the service of conquest, war, famine, and death. Humans may delight in (and profit from) the publishing success of apocalyptic fiction such as the *Left Behind* series. But Earth watches the drama unfold in real time, its future uncertain, save for the knowledge that suffering is happening *right now* and will continue to happen for generations to come. Thus, the preacher's proclamation about the certainty of God's presence, care, and desire for justice is all the more necessary.

NOT OUR FIRST APOCALYPTIC RODEO

While the writers of apocalyptic texts did not face the global scale of environmental, socioeconomic, cultural, military, and institutional pressures that, for us, seem to have reached their breaking point, they did face their own version of a cataclysmic collision of these forces. Sumney's descriptions of the circumstances faced by the oppressed people to whom these apocalyptic texts were written will be found throughout this book. As we will see, whether at the mercy of ancient rulers or our current neoliberal-industrial-capitalistic-military complex, those caught in the totality of empire find themselves desperate for release. We can understand, then, the need to turn to apocalyptic texts and the feelings that these texts want to address—hopelessness, panic, foreboding, frustration, helplessness, and perhaps even suicidal despair. These are the feelings that the preacher will need to be aware of when crafting sermons that address biblical passages about end times and the coming of divine judgment.

Yet the preacher will also recognize that not all people experience these feelings. Some try to numb them through artificial, chemical, or technological escapes. Others just appear to be happily oblivious—especially if their positions of privilege within the empire are comfortably (if temporarily) maintained. Thus, the preacher will likely face a congregation whose folks are not in agreement about the state of the world. Some will resist sermons that courageously and prophetically name what is happening. Others may have already given up hope. But there will also be those who are looking to the Word of God for something, anything, that helps them make sense of the chaos and disintegration that they see happening around them. The sermon can help create meaning by pointing to the ancient wisdom of these apocalyptic texts and drawing out implications for what we face today.

Even those who are comfortable—or comfortably numb—with the state of the world cannot deny that the culture itself is littered with "texts" that depict apocalyptic and post-apocalyptic futures. There is a plethora of books, movies, television shows, graphic novels, and video games that traffic in the images and story lines of end-of-the-world scenarios. *The Road* by Cormac McCarthy, *The Hunger Games* by Suzanne Collins, *The Maze Runner* by James Dashner, *Divergent* by Veronica Roth, and *The Handmaid's Tale* by Margaret Atwood; movies such as *Blade Runner, Mad Max, The Matrix,* and the animated *WALL-E*; video games like *Call of Duty, Half Life,* and *Fall Out;* television shows such as *The Last Man on Earth;* comics like *The Walking Dead* (also a television series)—all of them present a vision of the future that eerily echoes biblical themes and scenes from apocalyptic texts.

For preachers, these cultural texts cut both ways. On the one hand, one need only refer to a popular scene from one of these movies or books for contemporary hearers to tune in with recognition. Threatening skies, zombies roaming the streets, anarchy, mayhem, violence, desolation, and shortages of food and water in contemporary literature and movies seem to be lifted right from Daniel 9 or the book of Revelation (minus the zombies). But the preponderance of these modern dystopias presents two serious barriers for Christians to hear the biblical texts. First, in nearly all of these dystopias, evil wins. In fact, it appears that the genres themselves inadvertently create a self-fulfilling prophecy. The character Nix in the movie *Tomorrowland* explains why the messages of doom can backfire:

> [I believed] the only way to stop [the annihilation] was to show it. To scare people straight. Because what reasonable human being wouldn't be galvanized by the potential destruction of everything they've ever known or loved? To save civilization, I would show its collapse. But how do you think this vision was received? How do you think people responded to the prospect of imminent doom? They gobbled it up like a chocolate eclair! They didn't fear their demise, they re-packaged it. It could be enjoyed as video games,

The Challenges—And Opportunities—of Apocalyptic Preaching

as TV shows, books, movies, the entire world wholeheartedly embraced the apocalypse and sprinted towards it with gleeful abandon.[13]

This is exactly what we want to avoid in preaching apocalyptic texts from the Bible. When visions of fantastical beasts, death, destruction, and doom show up in Scripture, they are not intended to be repackaged as products for consumption, as has been done with the lucrative *Left Behind* series. Rather, their function is to tell a different story, which is that even if this is where we are now—heading toward the worst case scenario—God does not abandon the world or us. What we see, and what the proclamations of doom envision, are not the last word.

To this, modern listeners may respond, "Of course! That's where the hero comes in!" Within nearly every one of the secular stories of the apocalyptic genre there is the singular hero, perhaps with a small band of friends, who finds a way to survive, beat back the zombies, find a cure, or unlock the secret to a better future. They battle sadistic rulers, savage creatures, double-crossing fellow survivors, and the destitution of Earth, to emerge with a glimmer of hope for humanity. These stories have strong appeal, but they are based on a dangerous premise, which is that the salvation of humanity and the world is up to the individual. The theological premise of these genres is that we are alone, abandoned by God (if there ever was one), and the fate of the world rests in our hands. The best we can hope for are a few loyal and ingenious friends to accompany us as we make our way in this grave new world.

This premise of the apocalyptic hero throws up the second barrier to preachers trying to proclaim—and listeners trying to hear—the gospel in end-times texts. The hero trope is antithetical to the intention of apocalyptic texts in the Bible for two reasons. First, Scripture promises that we are not alone, and that even if we fail, God does not. Second, apocalyptic texts in Scripture are not about singular individuals; they are about the community of the faithful who are strengthened and upheld by a divine and benevolent force bigger than themselves. In contrast, the modern day concept of the hero and a band of fellow stalwart survivors battling for survival is like a flame drawing moths. We are seduced by something that distracts us and draws away our energy that is needed for something far more important—building faith and building community. Thus, sermons based on apocalyptic texts will need to reveal the problematic nature of

---

13. Bird, *Tomorrowland*.

secular doomsday dramas while clearly pointing the way to the true light of the gospel.

Yet even while the preacher is countering the distracting messages of the apocalypse in popular culture, there is an even more daunting task—refuting the dangerous "Rapture theology" of Christian millennialism.

LEAVING BEHIND *LEFT BEHIND*

When I was nine years old in the late '70s, a friend of mine and her family took me to their church to see a movie. I was very excited because I loved going to movies, and I thought it was cool that a church was going to show a real movie with popcorn and candy! But when we got to the church and descended the steps to the basement, I realized I was going to be disappointed. There was no popcorn, no candy. Only rows of hard metal chairs facing a screen.

My disappointment turned to fear as I watched the film. It was a movie about the end of days and what was going to happen when Jesus came back to Earth. It was terrifying! It showed images of the moon turning the color of blood, the sun going dark, and stars falling from the sky. It painted a picture of mass confusion on Earth, with people running around in sheer terror as Jesus comes down in a great cloud of doom. The movie followed the story of one family's trials and tribulations, including watching their young son being tortured by agents of the Antichrist.

After it was over, my friend's parents asked me what I thought of the movie. I said that I thought it was really scary and that I was worried that maybe the end of the world would happen while I was alive. They told me that everything I saw in the movie was in the Bible and is exactly the way things are going to happen when Jesus comes back. "You should be worried," they said. "Everyone should be worried about Jesus coming again."

This was the same message I received from the books given to me by members of my extended family who attended churches where authors like Frank Peretti, Tim LaHaye, and Jerry Jenkins were read with as much fervor as the Bible. Books like Peretti's *This Present Darkness* and LaHaye and Jenkins's *Left Behind* series put the fear of God and angels into my nightmares and daydreams. When I think back on the way these books and movies created such dread of Jesus in my impressionable young mind, it's a wonder I didn't run screaming from the church and the Bible. Instead, by the grace of God, it led me into a lifelong pursuit of theological and biblical study that eventually resulted in my becoming a pastor and seminary professor of preaching and worship. Something in my head and heart told me that what they were showing me in that cold, dark church basement and in those terrifying books was not the Jesus and God of the Bible. I had to find different answers and wrestle with these biblical passages in other contexts in order to get a fuller understanding of what they mean for our lives.

But for millions of people, Christian apocalyptic fiction is not a genre to be critically examined; it is akin to the Bible itself. An entire multimillion-dollar industry has been created around graphic Christian horror that grips the faithful in fear and fantasy. Worse, it peddles a narrative that supports a political agenda of war-making in the Middle East, environmental degradation, patriarchal control over women and their bodies, and anti-Semitic and Islamophobic white nationalism. Eighty million copies of the Left Behind books, along with numerous Rapture websites, movies, and spin-offs threaten to drown out the gospel of hope, renewal, and love. Meanwhile, the preacher on a Sunday morning has about fifteen to twenty minutes to proclaim that Jesus' return is about justice, transformation, and healing. So it's important to make these sermons count for deconstructing harmful theology and reconstructing a theology of nonviolence and an ethic of care for those most vulnerable.

These distorted fundamentalist end-time narratives pose the opposite problem of secular doomsday products. They insist that the state of the world *is* God's will. The suffering endured by people and the planet is the result of God's wrath against the heathens, and, worse, it is inevitable. Those ascribing to this theology assent to the suffering of others (and even their own suffering) because they see no possibility for a better future until they are whisked away by a vengeful God smiting the Earth and all his (sic) enemies. In both secular and Christian apocalyptic fiction, however, the result is the same. People resign themselves to having no agency in God's work of restoration. Or, worse, they believe that polluting the Earth or stirring up war in the Middle East is going to speed up Christ's return.

Preachers, then, have a profound challenge—to reintroduce their listeners to the apocalyptic texts in a way that takes them on a journey that is different from either the secular or fundamentalist Christian paths. It is not a journey that leads to war or ecological collapse or oppressive dystopias, but rather "a journey into the heart of God, a journey into the heart of our world," says Rossing. Apocalyptic texts give us a way of seeing that "teaches us how to look at the stories of our lives and the structures of violence and power in light of God's shepherding Lamb. It teaches us to challenge oppression and to look for signs of hope, even when evil seems overpowering. It gives us an urgent vision for our future in which God dwells with us, on earth."[14] And it invites us to actively participate in that future in a life-giving way.

HOMILETICAL ORIENTATION

The sermons in this book will be grounded in a theology of preaching wherein "the Word of God spoken is itself the Word of God in preaching or God's own speech to us. Thus preaching has a dual aspect: divine activity and human activity, God's Word and human speech."[15] This dual function of preaching emphasizes both the human activity of the preacher who takes the suffering of humanity and Earth into consideration when proclaiming God's Word, as well as God's action of calling people to awareness, repentance, and hope in the midst of despair. Such proclamation is enhanced by engaging with other dialogue partners, as Richard Lischer states: "Beyond the preacher's pastoral experiences lies theology's perennial dialogue with psychotherapy, anthropology, philosophy, ideology, politics, the arts, science, medicine, cybernetics, and ethics. This dialogue not only informs preaching; it makes it possible—and intelligible."[16]

As a Lutheran homiletician, my commitment to preaching both Law and Gospel will likely be evident in many of the sermons. Martin Luther taught that God's Law drives us to the gospel of Jesus Christ. Gospel without the Law leads to pablum and what Dietrich Bonhoeffer called "cheap grace."[17] But Law without Gospel leads to despair, fear, and hopelessness. Therefore, the Law-Gospel dialectic will be helpful for preaching about apocalyptic texts so that we are forthright about both individual and systemic sin but also the necessity and sureness of God's response of justice, grace, mercy, reconciliation, and a "new creation."

My homiletic is also strongly influenced by what John McClure identifies as a liberation theology approach to preaching, which develops "a profound awareness of Christ incarnate in the pain and suffering of the poor, the marginalized, the oppressed, the shamed, the shunned, the outcast,

---

14. Rossing, *The Rapture Exposed*, xviii.
15. Ngien, "Theology of Preaching in Martin Luther."
16. Lischer, *A Theology of Preaching*, 9.
17. Bonhoeffer, *The Cost of Discipleship*.

The Challenges—And Opportunities—of Apocalyptic Preaching

the abused, or the disenfranchised."[18] I extend this liberation theology to include an ecotheological orientation for preaching that moves to expand our awareness beyond the human community to embrace the other-than-human community of Earth-kin and Earth itself. Including these voices at the homiletical "round table" (to use McClure's and Lucy Atkinson Rose's phrase) arises out of, and is a natural extension of, the gospel's concern with "the least of these" and the good news about the coming of God's new creation. In the preacher's proclamation of grace within a sermon about apocalyptic texts, "God's will and power are identified not with what socially *is* but with what *will be*."[19]

Consider, for example, passages such as Isaiah 65:17–19, 2 Corinthians 5:17, and Revelation 21:15, each of which contain either the phrase "new heaven and new earth" or "new creation." A sermon about this theme will proclaim hope as "an absolutely fundamental theological category [because] anticipation of a new future grounded in faith in God conditions and motivates life," says McClure. "The Christian life is one of hope, consciousness-raising, learning from and suffering with the oppressed (in order to come close to Christ), hope for and involvement in the work of social transformation, and joy in the present, rooted in faith's hope for and vision of the future."[20] We'll explore this theme of hope and new creation more fully throughout the book.

Having traced the contours of the complexities that accompany preaching about apocalyptic texts, we can establish some parameters for apocalyptic preaching. A sermon that preaches both "law" about our crisis as well as "gospel" proclaiming God's grace in the midst of our failures finds a way to do three things. First, the sermon will honor the intrinsic value of God's Creation, inclusive of humanity. Second, the sermon will realistically state the dilemmas in which we find ourselves today and offer prophetic critique in order to participate in God's transformative justice. Third, the sermon will look to the crucifixion and resurrection of Jesus Christ for clues as to how we as the church might creatively live into the proleptic vision of Christ's return that leads to hope, restoration, and community.

Fundamentally, we hope that this book will bolster the confidence of the preacher to undertake apocalyptic preaching in the first place. As Philip

---

18. McClure, *Other-Wise Preaching*, 136.
19. McClure, *Other-Wise Preaching*, 137.
20. McClure, *Other-Wise Preaching*, 137.

Quanbeck notes, when it comes to preaching about apocalyptic passages in the Bible:

> The temptation is to avoid those texts altogether. The infrequent appearance of Revelation in the Revised Common Lectionary aids in that conspiracy of silence. If, however, there is something central to Christian theology in those apocalyptic texts, those texts need to be proclaimed. If the lectionary is not going to help, the preacher needs to do something intentional, such as a sermon series on apocalyptic texts. These texts cannot be left to the Christian fringe.[21]

We agree with Quanbeck's assertion that preachers must address apocalyptic texts in their sermons. Apocalyptic preaching attempts to answer the question, how shall we live in this space in between the already and the not yet?[22] How shall we sojourn in this "becoming" time and space that is so precariously perched upon the abyss? The fact is that chaos *does* bring pain and destruction with it. The "birth pangs" described by Paul in Romans 8 may be heralding a new creation, but the woman in travail must learn how to push through the pain and violent upheaval. Ideally, she will have midwives to coach her along, remind her to breathe, and guide the emergence of the new creation. Perhaps that is one role for the preacher—to serve as a midwife for God's people and Earth longing for the birth of the new creation.

This means that when we are preaching apocalyptic texts, we are on a kind of frontier, a liminal place between the Divine and the people. Thus we have a very important job, which is to help people keep God's horizon in sight. There is a tension between the immediate time and the eschatological time always coming to us from the horizon. As people are so caught up in the hurriedness and scatteredness of everyday profane living, the worship service and preaching help to bring the horizon of holiness back into our focus. The liturgy and sermon help to reorient us in time and to step back into that journey towards the eternal. God's horizon of holiness keeps calling to us.

As worship leaders and preachers, we hold these two edges together—the past and the present time—while also looking toward that horizon of the eschatological future. The poet David Whyte speaks of the "generous

---

21. Quanbeck, "Preaching Apocalyptic Texts," 318.

22. Margaret Swedish's book *Living Beyond the "End of the World"* offers a practical and cogent guide to this question.

The Challenges—And Opportunities—of Apocalyptic Preaching

surprise" that comes to us in good literature and art, and, I would add, in worship services and preaching.[23] This generous surprise brings us into a new world, but also a world that is familiar to us. It is the paradox of the crucified body resurrected—bearing the scars yet transformed by God's power and grace into new life. This is what apocalyptic preaching can do. It can guide us into a world where we are changed when we come into this generous surprise. Apocalyptic preaching invites transformation, and transformation happens primarily to those who are paying attention. The more deeply we attend to what is being revealed to us, the more our hearts are broken and our minds are resolved to act. You as a worship leader and preacher are the one who can help to communicate this to your congregation and to a world that is desperately in need of vision.

The challenge, Catherine Keller says, is "how to begin. Again. Amidst every kind of loss."[24] Preaching apocalyptic texts proclaims that it is God's love that hovers and dances, breathes and laughs as the *ruach-spirit* upon the abyss. It is love that submerges and reemerges from the depths. It is love that creates. It is love that becomes one of us in this powerful, fragile humanity. "[T]o love is to bear with the chaos."[25] Love attends the crucifixion and does not look away. Love brings balm and burial spices to the tomb of a crucified Earth. And love stands in the garden, gasping in wide-eyed recognition of the stranger, our teacher the Rabbi—the beloved new creation calling our name.

---

23. Whyte, *What to Remember When Waking*.
24. Keller, *Face of the Deep*, 158.
25. Keller, *Face of the Deep*, 29.

Chapter 3

Daniel 7:13, 15–18

¹*In the first year of King Belshazzar of Babylon, Daniel had a dream and visions of his head as he lay in bed. Then he wrote down the dream:* ²*I, Daniel, saw in my vision by night the four winds of heaven stirring up the great sea,* ³*and four great beasts came up out of the sea, different from one another. . . .* ¹⁵*As for me, Daniel, my spirit was troubled within me, and the visions of my head terrified me.* ¹⁶*I approached one of the attendants to ask him the truth concerning all this. So he said that he would disclose to me the interpretation of the matter:* ¹⁷*"As for these four great beasts, four kings shall arise out of the earth.* ¹⁸*But the holy ones of the Most High shall receive the kingdom and possess the kingdom forever—forever and ever."*

AN EXEGESIS OF DANIEL 7

Jerry L. Sumney

Daniel is the only book in the Hebrew Bible whose literary form is apocalyptic. There are other books that employ apocalyptic imagery and participate, at least in part, in apocalyptic's understanding of reality, but only Daniel is a fully apocalyptic writing. Many agree that it is the first Jewish book written in full apocalyptic style. It is also a book that provoked a good bit of interest in the first centuries of its existence. This can be seen not only

Daniel 7:13, 15–18

from the many quotations from and allusions to it in the New Testament, but also by the fact that three additions to it written in Greek are found in the Apocrypha.

The main character of this book, Daniel, is presented as a person who lived during the time of the exile, that is after the nation of Judah fell and the population was deported to Babylon (today's Iraq). Judah had been a vassal of Babylon since about 605 BCE. But when King Jehoiakim saw difficulties mounting between Egypt and Babylon, he declared independence for Judah in 598. He died before king Nebuchadnezzar arrived, but his son (Jehoiachin) was defeated and, along with others of the royal family and leading citizens, deported to Babylon. So the initial wave of the exile began in 597. Jehoiachin's uncle, Zedekiah, was left in charge of Judah and finally was convinced to establish an alliance with Egypt and revolt against the Babylonians in 589. After an eighteen-month siege, Jerusalem fell and most inhabitants of the city who were left alive were exiled to Babylon in 587. The exile ended nearly fifty years later when Cyrus allowed the Jews to return home in 538.

While this is the period in which the stories in Daniel are set, this is not the era in which the book was composed. Daniel was written in the second century BCE, at the time of the Maccabean revolt. This can be seen from the Greek loan words found in Daniel and from the author's knowledge of the Greek period. His descriptions of events in the period after Alexander the Great (d. 322 BCE) are better than those of the previous Persian and Babylonian periods. The stories about Daniel's life in Babylon in chapters 2—6 almost certainly existed prior to their inclusion in this book, perhaps even in written form.

The stories and visions brought together in Daniel are intended to help the readers endure the persecution inflicted by Antiochus IV, king of the Seleucid (Syrian) Empire 175–164/3 BCE. Late in 167 Antiochus outlawed Judaism in Judea. He took this step because some of its inhabitants had insistently rejected Hellenization, seeing it as a violation of their religion. This religious conviction constantly made his ruling of Judea more difficult. He had tried offering citizenship to those who would Hellenize, but the rate of acceptance had been too low. Furthermore, when a rumor was circulated that Antiochus had been killed in a war with Egypt, a rebellion broke out in Jerusalem against the High Priest Menelaus, whom Antiochus had installed. When Roman intervention forced Antiochus to withdraw from Egypt, he marched on Jerusalem. He slaughtered thousands of its inhabitants, reestablished Menelaus as high priest, and stationed troops in Jerusalem. But the trouble did not stop, so in December of 167 he set up a statue of Zeus in the temple of God in Jerusalem and sacrificed a pig to Zeus there. Additionally, he outlawed keeping the Sabbath and circumcising children and he burned as many copies of the Law as he could find.

In the following days he decided all residents of Judea should be forced to break the Law. Many were tortured to death rather than deny their faith or violate the Law. Antiochus even sent soldiers to various cities with orders to force everyone, on threat of death, to offer incense to another god. When they arrived in the town of Modin, an old priest named Mattathias killed the first person who was willing to offer a sacrifice. He then escaped into the crowd. Our sources say he did this out of his "zeal for the Law" (1 Macc 2:23–26). This outstanding deed made him a figure around whom the scattered "pious" could rally. Mattathias died within a year of this act, but his son Judas succeeded him as leader of the movement. Using guerilla tactics, Judas and his followers retook the temple in three years. Their rededication of the temple to God is still remembered by the festival of Hanukkah.

It is probably after the desecration of the temple by Antiochus that Daniel was written. It was written to help those facing persecution or martyrdom remain faithful. Daniel's stories tell of others who had faced similar situations, who had been ordered to eat unclean food or not to pray to God. When the characters of the stories resist, God intervenes to help them. Such stories are intended to encourage obedience to the Law in these difficult times. Those reading Daniel in the midst of the Maccabean Revolt know that God is not saving their fellows from harm or death, but the stories still bring courage by letting them know that God could (and so might) intervene to save them. They reasoned that if God was not intervening, there must be a reason, perhaps the previous sins of the people. The visions that begin in chapter 7 of Daniel give another slant on why things are so bad for the people of God. This is an eschatological, apocalyptic explanation. This explanation allows that evil is reigning but asserts that God is about to overthrow that dominion.

The report of the vision in Daniel 7 is in the first person. This is common in apocalyptic writings. Before this point in Daniel, the stories have been in the third person. So the author of Daniel conforms to the style of apocalyptic writing when he turns to visions. Our lection is a part of Daniel's first vision, its introduction and the beginning of its interpretation. In this vision, Daniel sees four beasts rise out of the sea, that realm of chaos that is hostile to God. The four beasts come one after the other and eventually the ruling power of them all is taken away because of the judgment of the Ancient One and by the "one like a Son of Man" ("like a human being" in the NRSV; 7:13–14). The most attention is focused on the fourth beast, who provokes God to action by the arrogant speaking of one of its horns (7:7–10).

Each of these four beasts represents a kingdom. The sequence of kingdoms and kings found here conforms more closely to the biblical accounts of them than to any historical accounts. The first beast is like a lion with eagle's wings. This beast represents the Babylonian Empire. The presence of lions with wings on Babylonian temples and palaces indicates that this is the kingdom the author has in mind. Perhaps its being given the mind of a human alludes to the story of Nebuchadnezzar being given a human mind after living as an animal for "seven times" (ch. 4). Its wings being plucked may point to the encroachment of the Persian Empire on the Babylonian Empire. The second beast was like a bear. This beast represents the Medes, particularly in the person of Darius (6:1), who ruled after Nebuchadnezzar. The third beast, which was like a leopard with four heads and four wings, is the Persian Empire.

The fourth beast is yet more terrifying and powerful than the previous beasts. It has no parallel among creatures, with its iron teeth and its crushing of things under its feet. This beast represents Alexander the Great (d. 322 BCE) and the empire he established. Alexander's empire encompassed all the other three, which were left as insignificant or as vassals. The ten horns of this beast represent either ten kings within one line (the Seleucids) of the kingdoms that developed after Alexander's death and the break-up of the empire or, as many scholars now think, kings of ten other countries who ruled at the time of Antiochus IV. If this latter view is correct, then the three horns he removes are three kings Antiochus defeated in battle. We are not told at this point what arrogant things this horn speaks, but whatever it says provokes God to act, to sit in court as judge.

The judgment scene is a theophany that draws on images of God as warrior and as judge (7:9–14). God's white clothing may point to God's holiness or purity. God's white hair may point to the same characteristics but also to longevity or eternity. The fire that is all about God is a common feature of theophanies in the Hebrew Bible. That the throne is presented on wheels is probably drawn directly from Ezekiel 1. The description of the throne may draw on the image of a war chariot and so further combine

God's roles as sovereign judge and warrior. God is also surrounded by thousands of attendants, perhaps pointing to God's majesty, as God enters into judgment.

In God's judgment the arrogant horn is put to death and the other beasts are rendered powerless. But this is not all! The final result is that "one like a son of man" or "like a human being" appears in the clouds and establishes the rule of God that is to last forever (7:13–14). It is interesting to note the contrast between the origin of the beasts and that of the "one like a human being." The beasts rise from the chaotic and God-opposing sea, while the "one like a human being" comes from the from clouds of heaven and thus perhaps represents conforming to the will of God. And, of course, the latter is the successful force in the vision.

As one might expect, this vision troubles Daniel. The second part of our lection has him ask one of God's court attendants what this vision means. He is told that the four beasts represent four kings (v. 17). Here the kings represent kingdoms, just as Nebuchadnezzar represented the kingdom of Babylon in the statue which appeared in his dream in chapter 2 (see vv. 37–38). These beasts are specifically identified as kingdoms in 7:23. Daniel is particularly interested in the fourth beast, especially in the horn that spoke arrogantly. We are given more detail about the activities of this ruler beginning in v. 21, where we are told that he made war against the holy ones and was winning. This condition continued until God intervened in judgment and the kingdom of God was established.

After this brief description of what Daniel saw, a poetic interpretation of the fourth beast and the arrogant horn follows (vv. 23–27). Again, the fourth beast is said to establish dominion over all the earth (v. 23). Then the arrogant one arises and we find out more precisely what actions he takes: he speaks against the most high, wears out the saints, and changes the religious calendar and the law (v. 25). Each of these actions, especially the last two, correspond to actions carried out by Antiochus at the time of the Maccabean Revolt. The first two are rather general but are certainly appropriate descriptions of the desecration of the temple and the persecution of the faithful. More specifically, Antiochus forbade the observance of Jewish festivals, including the Sabbath, and he tried to put an end to keeping the Law in Judea. We are also told that this horn will be successful at first, in fact, for three and a half years (a time plus two times plus a half time). It is after this amount of time that the Lord will sit in judgment and the horn (Antiochus) will be destroyed and the kingdom of God established (vv. 26–27).

This timetable comes fairly close to describing what actually happened in Judea. The Maccabean forces retook the Temple Mount in three years and rededicated it to the God of Israel. Antiochus IV died shortly after that. Unfortunately, that did not begin a period of peace, because Antiochus V also made war against Judas Maccabee and Jerusalem, though he did grant them some religious freedom. After the two-year reign of Antiochus V, the Maccabeans began to gain more political power and religious freedom until, ultimately, they declared independence for the Jewish state before the end of the second century BCE.

Daniel 7, then, speaks to a specific situation in which the faithful of God are suffering persecution precisely because they are being faithful to the Law of God. These were desperate times when faithfulness could entail torture or death, and often did. The situation looked hopeless. The Maccabeans looked impossibly outnumbered and out-armed. What are the people of God to do? What does such a situation say about the power and goodness of God? This vision and its interpretation encourage the readers to remain faithful to God because God will have the last word. God is about to act as judge on those who are persecuting God's people, totally destroying them for their wickedness. Not only that, God will also grant an everlasting kingdom to the people of God (7:17–18). The roles will be reversed so that those now persecuted will reign and those now persecuting will serve those whom they previously troubled. Since v. 27 does not refer to a specific leader but grants the kingdom to the people of God as a whole, it may be that the "one like a human being" in v. 13 is to be understood symbolically as the people of God, just as the heavenly attendant calls the beasts kings, but means kingdoms. Whether that is the case or not, the point of this vision remains unchanged. The suffering faithful are assured of the judgment of the persecutors and are promised that the power and goodness of God will, in the end, prevail for the good of the people of God. It is important to recognize that all of this activity is presented as an act of God. This is not something the people of God can accomplish on their own. The beast is too powerful for the people to defeat; only God can provide this relief and make these blessings a reality.

The lectionary text for All Saints Day in Year C intends the focus to be on vv. 17–18 where the faithful live forever in God's kingdom. This is important for Daniel's original readers because it encourages them to be faithful in the midst of persecution. It says that whatever happens to them now is not the last word and that their persecutors will not get away with what they are doing. God's coming in judgment will set things right. While few Christians today face such persecution, this passage can still provide the assurance that the faithful who die abide in the place where God's will is fully realized.

Daniel 7:13, 15–18

IDEAS FOR PREACHING

Leah D. Schade

Mind-mapping the images of Daniel 7

For those who follow the Revised Common Lectionary, the pericope for this Sunday, All Saints Day, contains only verses 13 and 15–18 of chapter 7, most likely to emphasize verse 18. This verse has the most relevance for the theme of remembering those who have died: "But the holy ones of the Most High shall receive the kingdom and possess the kingdom for ever—for ever and ever." Certainly it is necessary to highlight the promise that the saints whose lives we mourn are in the presence of God. However, what this pericope leaves out are eleven verses of vivid imagery from Daniel's apocalyptic vision. The preacher might consider having these verses included during the reading in the worship service in order to provide more context and explore the rich symbolism.

Helping listeners see the parallels between the world of the text, the world of the original listeners, and their own world will yield a plethora of images for preaching. In her book *Finding Language and Imagery*, Jennifer Lord encourages preachers to study the words and images of the biblical text in order to do a deep dive into both the nouns and the verbs of the passage. She suggests creating a "mind map" of certain words and images in order to help us "sift through our ideas for a sermon and hone a claim," as well as generate and expand our thinking "to make associations that are necessary for preaching to engage real life."[1]

A mind map of Daniel's depictions of the four beasts terrorizing the Earth and God's faithful people may point to modern-day examples of communities suffering from the effects of "beasts" such as the opioid crisis, police brutality, systemic racism, or the climate crisis, for example. Using vivid words, connecting with the senses, and even drawing on popular culture can establish salience with the metaphor of the "beasts" as a symbol of hegemonic powers bent on destruction.

---

1. Lord, *Finding Language and Imagery*, 39.

Apocalypse When?

Considering different forms for a sermon on Daniel 7

When thinking about the sermon's form, three approaches stand out as strong possibilities. One is Eugene Lowry's "homiletical plot" sequence, which draws on the classic plot form for a dramatic story: disruption, complication, clue to resolution, experience of the good news, and resolution toward a new future.[2] Daniel 7 contains the elements of this sequence, in that Daniel's sleep is disturbed by a dream, he is overwhelmed by the vision of the beasts, but then glimpses "the Ancient One" enthroned for judgment. He experiences the good news upon seeing the Son of Man descending, and finally experiences resolution with the assurance that the "holy ones" will be with God and that God's reign will depose the forces of the evil. The sermon could develop this sequence on two parallel tracks by showing how the vision mirrors the experiences of the besieged Israelites and how they drew strength from Daniel's apocalyptic dream. As Sumney noted above, "This explanation allows that evil is reigning but asserts that God is about to overthrow that dominion." The sermon can conclude with a reminder on this All Saints Sunday that all those who have died in the faith are in the presence of the Ancient One, and that our own destiny is similarly assured. This, in turn, gives us strength to resist the beastly powers of our own time and trust in the providence of God.

A second option is to focus on the cycle of the liturgical year that brings us to this All Saints Sunday and how it contrasts with the hegemonic powers of empire that seek to desecrate our sacred spaces and sacred times, just as the "beasts" do in Daniel. In this sermon, connecting the dots between the story of Daniel in Babylon with the story of the Maccabean revolt against the desecration of the temple can help listeners draw comparisons to the ways in which sacred time and space is stripped away today. Even our times of mourning are cut short in this culture; we are rushed to "move on" when someone has died. This is why the honoring of liturgical time and a day like All Saints is so important. When we worship, when we observe the sabbath, when we practice the rituals of the cyclical year, we are, in fact, resisting the powers that want to strip time of its sacredness and turn it into a commodified product. The lighting of candles in memory of our loved ones, the breaking of the bread and sharing of the cup, the singing of hymns that have lasted the test of time—these are all ways in which the Ancient

---

2. Lowry, *The Homiletical Plot*.

Daniel 7:13, 15–18

One is enthroned within our midst, driving out the beasts, and surrounding us with the witness of the saints.

In the sermon that follows, you'll see an example of another form—the chiastic structure. This is a technique where a pattern of ideas in the first half is mirrored in the second half, but in reverse order. For example, Idea 1 is followed by Idea 2, pivots at Idea 3, then moves back to Idea 2 then 1. In this way, the beginning and ending of the sermon contain "book-ends"—a story or concept introduced at the beginning that is recapitulated at the end. This sermon, "Saints and Monsters: *Stranger Things* Meets Daniel 7," is a loose chiastic structure:

A1 *Stranger Things*

    B1 Monsters in culture, monsters in Daniel

        C Monsters close to home/All Saints

    B2 Defeating monsters in culture, defeating monsters in Daniel

A2 *Stranger Things*

Apocalypse When?

"MONSTERS AND SAINTS: *STRANGER THINGS* MEETS DANIEL 7"

A Sermon on Daniel 7:1–3, 15–18

Leah D. Schade

(This sermon was preached at St. Thomas Lutheran Church in Richmond, Kentucky, on All Saints Sunday, 2019.)

A twelve-year-old boy named Will Beyers is biking home at night when he sees a shadowy, not-quite-human figure appear out of nowhere right in front of him on the road. Will veers into the woods and his bike crashes to the ground. He gets up and catches a glimpse of the creature. It resembles one of the monsters in the Dungeons and Dragons game he had just been playing with his friends, a creature called the Demogorgon.

Will starts running through the woods to his home. Surely he'll be safe there. But no one is home. He is alone and the monster is after him.

He runs to the shed behind the house to find something with which to defend himself. He hears the growl of the monster as the light bulb above his head surges with light. He looks up to the ceiling, his eyes wide with fear.

And then he is gone. Vanished. Not a trace.

Has Will been kidnapped? Is he hiding? Is he lost? Is he dead?

These are the questions we're left with at the end of the first episode of a television series called *Stranger Things*.[3] It takes place in the fictional town of Hawkins, Indiana, in 1983. I started watching because my kids raved about the show, and because I like the cultural references to the eighties, the era in which I grew up. I came for the eighties, but I stayed for the drama.

Stranger Things is a suspenseful story about characters who must battle monsters from an alternate dimension called "the Upside Down." It's a world like ours, but it is filled with hideous creatures, toxic air that poisons the body, and a malevolent force called the Mind Flayer that controls all the beasts and is intent on destroying humanity. Government scientists, as well as the Russian military, create a gateway into this underworld, thinking they can control these evil forces to use for their own gain. What they discover is that they have unleashed a power that they cannot control, a

---

3. Duffer and Duffer, *Stranger Things.*

Daniel 7:13, 15–18

power that overtakes them and the unwitting citizens of Hawkins, growing and killing as it goes.

In *Stranger Things* I see a metaphor for the evil forces that threaten us and our children. Things like gun violence, drug addiction, and climate change. Not to mention the ill-fated efforts of some of our leaders who think they can consort with evil for their own personal gain. In all of these cases, when we mess around with malevolent forces thinking we can use them to gain power, we find we have unleashed something that we cannot control, a power that overtakes us and the people around us, growing and killing as it goes.

Why am I'm thinking about all of this? Because it's the season of monsters.

Halloween is the time of year when we hear tales about vampires, werewolves, and zombies. All Hallows Eve, as it was known in earlier times, is when the ghosts of the dead are believed to rise and torment the living. We revel in stories of demonic creatures wreaking mayhem because these tales tap into primordial fears and archetypal symbols that are as old as the shadows of our ancient cave-dwelling ancestors.

Now, you might think it's a bit unusual to talk about monsters in a sermon in a Christian church. But in our reading today on All Saints Sunday (the counter to Halloween), we hear about monsters. In fact, the Bible contains many references to monsters. This reading from the book of Daniel is just one example.

The seventh chapter tells about "four great beasts" that arise from the sea. These are truly "stranger things." One looked like a lion with wings like an eagle. Another was like a bear with three tusks in its mouth. A third was like a leopard with wings and four heads. The fourth was the most terrifying of all, a beast with ten horns: "It had great iron teeth and was devouring, breaking in pieces, and stamping what was left with its feet."

Why, you may wonder, is the Bible talking about monsters?

Monsters are mythical creatures symbolizing that which terrifies and terrorizes us. Whether it's the Demogorgon of *Stranger Things*, or Grendel in the medieval story of *Beowulf*, or the beast with ten horns in the book of Daniel, these monsters represent forces of incredible malevolent power. They show up in our nightmares, in the scary costumes we wear on Halloween, and the frightening stories we tell around campfires.

Monsters hide in the shadows, stalking us, waiting to jump out when we least expect it and tear us limb from limb. They feed on the weak, overpower the strong, and threaten to destroy the world as we know it.

But here's the thing. As much as we fear and loathe them, we need these stories about monsters.

I know, this probably seems like a strange thing to say. But the author of Daniel knew that writing about these monsters serves a purpose. It gives us a way to talk about the forces of evil so that our minds can comprehend them and we can mentally, physically, and spiritually prepare ourselves to face them, even if it scares us to do so. Let me explain.

The book of Daniel is what scholars call "apocalyptic," which in Greek means "unveiling" or "revealing." Apocalyptic literature is a genre that is characterized by mysterious visions, vivid imagery, and heart-stopping drama about the battle between good and evil. In the Bible, when a person receives a vision or dream like this, they are shown what is going on in the cosmic war between God and God's enemies. But the message comes by way of coded imagery that they, and we, have to decipher. The most well-known book of this kind is Revelation, but apocalyptic writings are found throughout the Bible, including this book of Daniel in the Hebrew Scriptures.

So, what is the purpose of these apocalyptic writings?

They are written to help those who are suffering under persecution. The monsters described in the book represent the empires, rulers, and armies that are oppressing people and destroying their communities, their sacred places, and their land. The setting of Daniel is during the exile in the Babylonian empire, but it was actually written when the Israelites were besieged by the Greeks, hundreds of years later. The book of Daniel is meant to bolster the faith of the Israelites who are watching their temple being desecrated, their people being tortured, and their worship practices outlawed. Hearing the stories of Daniel being protected by God in the lions' den and saved from the fiery furnace reminds them that God is with them when they face persecution. And these apocalyptic dreams proclaim who is truly sovereign over even the most powerful kings. It is the God of Israel, the Ancient One, the creator of heaven and earth, and the judge who commands all righteousness and brings down the evil ones.

Of course, not all apocalyptic stories have religious roots. But even if they aren't specifically about God, you can see the apocalyptic aspect of many well-known books, movies, and TV shows. Because they reveal a truth about our world and our struggles that can give us strength to engage the forces of evil.

J. K. Rowling's *Harry Potter* series, for example, was an extended metaphor about fighting fascism and authoritarian dictators. Suzanne Collins explained that her series *The Hunger Games* was meant to show us the truth about our consumerist culture that sacrifices children, oppresses entire communities, and sets us on a path to war, poverty, and environmental devastation. Likewise, when I watch *Stranger Things*, I see the monsters as a metaphor for the ways in which our children are being violently snatched into a world of the "Upside Down." Like the gun massacres that turn their schools into death zones. And environmental toxins and climate disruption that threatens to overtake our planet and their future.

But others may see something different when they look at those monsters, something more personal. They may recognize the kind of struggle that hits closer to home. Sometimes the monster is the cancer that is attacking the body. The bully at school or at work who is making your life miserable. The depression that lurks like an invisible demon. The Alzheimer's disease that is taking over a loved one's brain. The freak car accident that snatches away the life of someone we love.

The monsters are as varied as each of our experiences. So we need tools, weapons of the spirit (as Paul called them) to engage these monsters. And we need stories of people who have faced these creatures so that we can learn how to overcome them as well.

Some tales, like Beowulf, tell us that it is the singular hero outfitted with the fiercest weapons and strongest armor that can defeat the monsters. Other stories like *Stranger Things* suggest that the best way to fight the monsters is with a small band of friends that we can trust to look out for us. Each person brings their unique gifts and skills to the battle and bolsters the courage of their friends.

But other stories expand that circle to include a much larger group coming together. *The Lord of the Rings*, *The Hunger Games*, and the *Harry Potter* series show us that when a whole community is able to work together, they have a much wider network with which to fight the monsters. They find ways to communicate with each other and share information (often through secret codes). They teach and equip each other for the battle. And they share common values such as loyalty, bravery, and a commitment to truth and goodness. This enables them to withstand the assaults of a president and his mutated monsters in *The Hunger Games*. Or Sauron and his Orcs in Tolkien's legends. Or Voldemort and his demonic minions in *Harry Potter*.

The apocalyptic stories of the Bible, however, add an even deeper and more powerful dimension—that of divine intervention. As the passage in Daniel makes clear, it is only God who can ultimately defeat the monsters. In Daniel, God is called the "Ancient One" who sits on a throne of judgement surrounded by holy fire and deposes the monsters. Then "the Son of Man," the human being (whom Christians understand to be Jesus), descends from the clouds and the holy ones of God are finally given peace.

On this All Saints Sunday, we remember the holy ones who fought their own monsters. We are assured that "the holy ones of the Most High shall receive the kingdom and possess the kingdom for ever—for ever and ever."

This is God's love—as fierce as Will Beyers's mother who never, not for one moment, gives up looking for her son. As steadfast as Will's friends who never, not for one moment, allow their fears to overcome their courage on behalf of their friend. As loyal as Will's brother, Jonathan, who arms himself to battle the Demogorgon. And as miraculous as a twelve-year-old girl called El who has mysterious powers to help rescue Will, defeat the monster, and send it back to the Upside-Down.

Our God is all of this and more. For we know that no matter what battles we are fighting, no matter what monsters attack, no matter what demons we face, and no matter what happens to us on this side of the story, God will have the last word. The lost child will be found. The victims of the monsters will abide with God. And the forces of evil will be vanquished.

This is the story I need to hear, the story I need my children to hear, in as many ways as we can find. It's the story of monsters and the saints of God. This is our church's story. It's my story and your story. It's our story. Thanks be to God.

Chapter 4

Mark 13:24–37

(Year B—Advent—First Sunday in Advent)

²⁴"But in those days, after that suffering,
the sun will be darkened,
 and the moon will not give its light,
²⁵and the stars will be falling from heaven,
and the powers in the heavens will be shaken.
²⁶Then they will see 'the Son of Man coming in clouds' with great power and glory. ²⁷Then he will send out the angels, and gather his elect from the four winds, from the ends of the earth to the ends of heaven.
²⁸"From the fig tree learn its lesson: as soon as its branch becomes tender and puts forth its leaves, you know that summer is near. ²⁹So also, when you see these things taking place, you know that he is near, at the very gates. ³⁰Truly I tell you, this generation will not pass away until all these things have taken place. ³¹Heaven and earth will pass away, but my words will not pass away.
³²"But about that day or hour no one knows, neither the angels in heaven, nor the Son, but only the Father. ³³Beware, keep alert; for you do not know when the time will come. ³⁴It is like a man going on a journey, when he leaves home and puts his slaves in charge, each with his work, and commands the doorkeeper to be on the watch. ³⁵Therefore, keep awake—for you do not know when the master of the house will come, in the evening, or at midnight, or at cockcrow, or at dawn, ³⁶or else he may find you asleep when he comes suddenly. ³⁷And what I say to you I say to all: Keep awake."

Apocalypse When?

AN EXEGESIS OF MARK 13

Jerry L. Sumney

Mark 13 is often called the "Synoptic Apocalypse." It has long been the subject of controversy because of its treatment of the fall of the temple and the end time in a single passage. To understand this passage well we need to examine both its literary form and its place within Mark.

In form, this chapter is more like a testament than other forms we find used in apocalyptic writings (e.g., a vision). This form is known from works written both before and after the writing of Mark. The *Testament of the Twelve Patriarchs*[1] contains several examples of this genre. These *Testaments* contain what is presented as some of the last words of these people of faith, though they were written centuries after these people had died. Such works reveal the theological and eschatological views of their later authors. Their primary concerns are things happening in the time of the actual writer, which are often addressed by presenting the issue in the form of predictions made by those who lived long ago. Mark presents the remarks of Jesus in chapter 13 as some of the last things Jesus says to his disciples before his death. Furthermore, the subject of this discourse, the fall of the temple, was an important matter for all church members when Mark was written.

Mark was written sometime just before or just after the fall of the temple in Jerusalem (70 CE). This was a traumatic event for both Jewish and Gentile church members. Jewish believers in Christ had continued to worship in the temple until its destruction (see e.g. Acts 2:46 and 21:17–36). Gentile believers also knew it as the only temple of the true God they had begun to worship. So, what are they to think when this temple is destroyed? Does it mean their God is not as powerful as they thought? Does it mean God rejects the Jews? What could this mean about use of the Hebrew Scriptures, the only Bible they had? How could the God of the whole cosmos allow the one temple dedicated to that God to be overrun? Does it mean that things have gotten so evil that the second coming of Christ is imminent?

Mark 11:11–13:37 is dedicated to interpreting the fall of the temple. Chapter 11:12–26 combines what is usually called Jesus' "Cleansing of the Temple" and the story of the cursing of the fig tree with a literary device known as intercalation, or the sandwich technique. This device puts together

---

1. This writing is found in the Pseudepigrapha.

two stories that are to be interpreted as a single unit.[2] The combination of these two stories shows that Mark does not see Jesus' actions in the temple with those selling animals for sacrifice and the currency exchange brokers as a cleansing of the temple, but rather as the closing of the temple. That is, Jesus declares that the temple's time has passed. Just as the cursed fig tree was out of season, so now the temple's season has passed. This understanding of Jesus' actions at the temple would help the church cope with the fall of the temple because it tells them that it has less significance than they were attaching to it. With these episodes Mark is asserting that Jesus recognized that the temple would fall soon and had himself initiated its closing.

Chapter 12 contains Jesus' exchanges with those in charge of the temple. Mark portrays them as insincere and dishonest. This supports Mark's position that the temple no longer functioned as the place of the special presence of God and thus its fall is not so devastating for the church.

Following his exchange with these leaders and his comments on their insincerity, Jesus leaves the temple for the last time. As he does, his disciples look back and comment on how large and magnificent the temple is. Jesus' immediate response is that the temple will be destroyed (13:12). This response causes the disciples consternation, but it should also function as a source of encouragement for Mark's readers, who have now experienced its fall (or know that it is about to fall). It should provide some comfort to them to know that, even before his death, Jesus knew this was to occur. So the question of whether the destruction of the temple is devastating for the church's faith has been addressed, but the question that remains is: What does the fall of the temple *mean*? Does it have eschatological significance? Mark 13 addresses this question.

Mark says that when some of the disciples were with Jesus alone, they asked him two questions about his prediction of the destruction of the temple: When will it happen? and What will the signs for it be? Jesus responds to the questions in reverse order, but answers neither. Instead he addresses the time of the end. Vv. 5–27 talk about signs of the end, while vv. 28–37 deal with the time of the end.

Chapter 13:58 begins Jesus' response. These verses describe the time of the Roman War in Judea (66—70 CE). The time described in these verses is a time of war, famine, and earthquake. It is the kind of situation in which believers hope for the direct intervention of God and look for the presence

---

2 For another example of Mark using this device see 5:21–43, where he combines the healing of Jairus's daughter with the healing of the woman with the hemorrhage.

of God in some overwhelming manifestation. These verses intimate that in the context of the terrible destruction brought by this war, some people had arisen claiming to be the messiah ("Many will come in my name and say, 'I am he!'"; v. 6). Perhaps they were members of the church or people who appealed to churches claiming to be the returned Messiah/Christ. Jesus exhorts these disciples not to believe in such people because as terrible as the Roman War would be, it was not a sign that the end was near—it is only the beginnings of the birth pangs (v. 8). So the first answer to the unasked question about signs of the end is that the Roman War was not one of them. Some writers suggest that this rejection of the Roman War as a sign that the end is near was intended to cool eschatological enthusiasm among Mark's readers. At the least it says that this event, though seen by some as such, was not an indication that the end is near.

Vv. 9–13 turn to the subject of persecution. From the earliest days of the church's existence, persecution had been seen as a sign that the end could not be far off. After all, if God is to remain just and loving, God must intervene to stop the pain of those who suffer because of their belief in God. Mark has Jesus predict that those who believe in him will be handed over to all kinds of judicial officials and bodies. Jesus does not say God will spare them, but rather that God will be with them in the midst of these persecutions. God's Spirit will sustain them through legal examination and probably torture, helping them to maintain their confession and express their faith so that they do not have to worry about what to say in defense of their faith.

These verses also indicate that the lives of these church members will be patterned after Jesus' life in some significant ways. Not only will they be persecuted, but just as Jesus was, they will be betrayed by those close to them. Some interpreters think Mark has in mind here believers who have been betrayed by other church members. It is possible that some had betrayed fellow believers to escape death or torture or because of theological differences. Whether such betrayals were occurring, we do not know, but Mark's community has experienced persecution and probably the betrayal of some members by people close to them.

This section may also intend to quell immediate eschatological expectations by saying that the gospel must be preached throughout the whole world before the end comes (v. 10). It is doubtful that this had been accomplished by the time Mark was written. The section ends by asserting that those who endure the persecution with faith will be saved. Thus it is an exhortation to faithfulness in the face of persecution. However, it does not make these persecutions a sign of the end. If anything, it puts off the end by requiring the gospel to be preached to all nations. So for the second time Mark has Jesus reject the notion that something that might well be seen as a sign of the end, and probably had been understood as such, was in fact not a sign. Rather than looking for the immediate end, they are to endure with faith.

Verses 14–23 turn attention back to the temple. This has often been seen as one of the most difficult sections of Mark 13 because of its enigmatic imagery and seemingly threatening tone. But if we remember the historical and literary context of Mark, it is less difficult. The first image in these verses which needs our attention is the "desolating sacrilege," or as it is better known from the KJV, "the abomination of desolation." Perhaps the first thing to notice is that Mark expected his alert readers to recognize this figure (or object) almost immediately. That is the meaning of the parenthetical remark, "let the reader understand" (v. 14). As in all apocalyptic texts, such imagery is used to point to persons or events that readers could recognize and identify. While the meaning of this symbol may have been clear to Mark's initial readers, it has been the object of much consternation and speculation since then. This is often the case because interpreters of this passage have sought to identify this person with someone in their own time in history rather than in Mark's time. But for this passage to be meaningful to Mark's readers, it had to be someone they knew, so it *must* refer to someone in the first century.

This "desolating sacrilege" is an image drawn from Daniel (9:27; 11:31; 12:11—the phrase, "let the reader understand" is also a way to direct the reader's attention to this literary allusion). In the context of Daniel, it refers to Antiochus IV Epiphanes (who ruled Syria 175–164/3 BCE). Antiochus defiled the temple by erecting a statue of Zeus in it and sacrificing a pig to that god in the temple. This desecration became a paradigm for those who would defile the temple or hinder Jews from practicing Judaism. The works that record the conflict between Antiochus IV and the Jews of Judea (1 and 2 Maccabees) are in the Septuagint. This Greek translation of the Hebrew Bible was the most commonly used version of the Bible in the early church. So when this image from Daniel is brought into Mark, the readers understand that the subject is the temple—especially the desecration of the temple. The two first-century options that seem most likely are the emperor Caligula and the Roman General (later to be emperor) Titus. In 40 CE,

Caligula decided to press the matter of emperor worship in Judea by erecting a statue of himself in the Jerusalem temple and having sacrifices made to him there. He was persuaded not to carry out this course of action and his four-year reign ended the next year. Thus the temple was not actually defiled.

The second, and more probable, option for identifying the "Desolating Sacrilege" is Titus. Titus was the son of Vespasian, the general in charge of the Roman army in Judea during the war that took place in 66–70 CE. While the war was in progress, Vespasian perceived that if he were to return to Rome, he could seize the position of emperor. He left for Rome to secure that position for himself and left his son Titus in charge of the war. Titus completed this task, including the siege and destruction of Jerusalem and the temple. Since he directed the destruction of the temple, he seems to be the most likely candidate. So vv. 14–23 are about the destruction of Jerusalem and the temple in 70 CE.

The description of the difficulties those in Jerusalem will have to endure during this time is frightful. Verse 19 again draws on Daniel (12:1) when it describes this time as the most difficult in the history of the world. The tribulations are so great that no one would survive except for the mercy of God, which is issued on behalf of the church to reduce the time of this terrible suffering. In these desperate circumstances, Mark's Jesus predicts again that people will appear claiming to be the Messiah (vv. 21–22). These false messiahs will be so convincing, Mark says, that even some church members will be tempted to follow them. But Mark says all such claims are to be rejected. So the terrible destruction of Jerusalem and the temple are not signs that Christ is returning. The false messiahs who even perform signs may say this is the time of the presence of the Messiah, but Jesus says in advance that it is not because the fall of the temple is not a sign of the end.

This passage does, however, give instructions about how to react to these times. In v. 23, the disciples are told to "be alert." This may have a double meaning. First, they need to be alert about the coming of the destruction of Jerusalem so they can escape it, as v. 14 tells them to flee to the mountains. But perhaps more importantly, this is an eschatological warning that calls on them to be alert about the real second coming and to be alert so they are not deceived by the false messiahs.

Mark has now had Jesus say that the Jewish War, persecution of his followers, and the destruction of Jerusalem and the temple are all *not* signs

Mark 13:24-37

of the second coming. Finally in vv. 24-27, Jesus turns to the end itself. Clearly it is to happen sometime after all the suffering associated with the fall of Jerusalem. These verses say that the coming of the Son of Man will take place in conjunction with cosmic portents. This is probably a way of saying that the whole of creation is involved with the coming of the Son of Man. This is not an event about which anyone will need to be told because everyone will see the Son of Man coming in the clouds and all the elect will be gathered to him. This ingathering of the people of God is probably seen as the fulfillment of the promises of God made to those in exile (see Deut 30:4; Isa 11:11, 16; 27:12; Ezek 39:27). This event is the opposite of the scattering of the exile, it is the reclamation of the people of God for God. So the coming of the Son of Man, as it is envisioned here, will be seen by all and will achieve the purposes of God.

Now if we return to the question, "What are the signs?," we still have no answer. The only sign that the End is coming is that the End begins. The things others had designated as signs that the End must be near—none of them are accepted as genuine signs. They are, rather, explicitly rejected as signs. So as Mark closes this discussion of the signs of the End, his message has been that there are no events in world history one can point to as clear evidence that the End is near. Not even the destruction of the temple is such a sign.

After Mark concludes that there are no certain signs of the End, he turns to the subject of the time of the End (vv. 28-37). In this section Jesus tells two parables and offers some comments on them. The first of these, the parable of the fig tree, compares the coming of the Son of Man to the sprouting of the fig tree in summer. When you see the leaves coming out, you know it is summer. Again, the point seems to be that there is no time to look for signs. When you see one, the time is already upon you. Verse 30 adds urgency to this matter by saying that these things will all happen during "this generation." The phrase "all these things" clearly refers to the coming of the Son of Man as well as the destruction of Jerusalem and the persecutions.

Of course, we know from our vantage point that the End did not come in the first century or in the time of that first generation of the church. Perhaps Mark intends "this generation" to refer to his readers rather than the generation of the apostles, but that does little to resolve the problem. The next verse may help us understand this passage a bit better. Verse 32 asserts that no one knows the time of the End except the Father; not even Jesus knows. If this is the case, how can Jesus assert in v. 30 that the End will happen in "this generation"? There is a tension between these two verses which can be important for maintaining an apocalyptic perspective. It is important that the end is soon ("in this generation") and that its exact time is not known. These two points together call on the readers to be in a constant state of readiness for the second coming. And that is the point emphasized in the following parable of the man who goes on a trip and leaves his slaves in charge of the household.

This second parable is introduced with the exhortation: "Beware, keep alert." The parable then goes on to say that the servants must constantly be ready for the master's return because they do not know when he will return. The parable is followed immediately by the exhortation, "Keep awake." So rather than giving a timetable or giving a list of signs to look for, Jesus tells the disciples to be ready always because the End will come suddenly. So Mark has moved the emphasis from the End coming quickly to the End coming *suddenly*. This is a subtle but very important shift. It turns one's attention away from trying to predict when the End will come to living in a constant state of readiness for it. Because the End will come suddenly, one must always keep her/his accountability to God in clear focus.

Mark wants to be certain that his readers understand that the exhortations drawn from these parables are as much for them as for the disciples on the Mount of Olives. So Jesus' last sentence in this discourse is directed, not to the disciples, but to the readers of Mark: "what I say to you [the disciples] I say to all: Keep awake." Thus, Mark's readers are exhorted to be ready always for the sudden coming of the Son of Man.

Mark 13 has taken us on a circuitous route. It begins with the prediction of the destruction of the temple, moves to the question of when that destruction will happen, then to discussion of the things which are not signs that the End is coming near (including the destruction of the temple), to comments about how sudden the End will be, and finally to an exhortation to be ready always for that sudden End. This passage accomplishes at least two functions in Mark. First, it completes Jesus' dealings with the temple, showing that its fall is no surprise and that it is not a portent of the End. Furthermore, the fall of the temple is not to be construed as a sign of God's weakness because it was known to Jesus and Jesus himself had announced the closing of the temple (ch. 11). Second, chapter 13 leads to the same goal we find for much apocalyptic writing. Its rhetoric, which culminates

Mark 13:24–37

by designating the End as sudden, is designed to exhort the readers to constant faithfulness in the face of persecution and the fall of the temple.

Apocalypse When?
IDEAS FOR PREACHING MARK 13:24-37

Leah D. Schade

Considering ministry context

In the verses prior to this pericope, Jesus describes a period of terrible suffering. So the preacher will want to ask, in what ways has the congregation and/or community experienced suffering? One of the most powerful things we can do as preachers is to name that suffering and then frame it within a biblical and theological context. In this way, those who have suffered will have the experience of being seen, being paid attention to, and being validated as worthy of God's care. By speaking forthrightly about suffering, the preacher can exercise what homiletician Dale Andrews called "prophetic care"—a way of understanding prophetic preaching as an *expression of pastoral care*.[3] Andrews saw pastoral care and prophetic proclamation not as two contrasting aspects of ministry, but as complementary and reinforcing of each other. Caring for one's congregation necessarily entails naming and calling out sin and suffering (including systemic sin) in a prophetic way. This prophetic voice, then, arises from a pastor's deep and empathetic—even suffering—love for God's people.

The preacher will also want to be attentive to social, national, and environmental contexts. What are current events or environmental news that may feel as if "the powers in the heavens" are being shaken? Because of the nature of instantaneous news feeds from around the world, the barrage of headlines can make it seem as if the "stars are falling from heaven." When natural disasters, wars, the effects of climate disruption, and health pandemics overwhelm us, sometimes biblical language found in passages such as Mark 13:24-37 is the only thing that captures the enormity of what we are experiencing.

This is why understanding the historical context of the passage can be especially helpful. Using Sumney's exegesis, we learn that the original readers/hearers of Mark's gospel were experiencing existential angst with the destruction of the temple. In the sermon, the preacher will want to explore

---

3. See Sheppard, Allen, and Ottoni-Wilhelm, eds., *Preaching Prophetic Care.*

what we can learn from that period of time that can shed light on our own period of upheaval.

Countering apocalyptic panic

The temptation for some who read these texts in light of current events is that they may latch onto them as portents of apocalyptic doom that can induce either paralyzing fear or susceptibility to those who profit from manipulating such fear. This manipulation may manifest in any number of ways, including obeisance to militant strongmen and authoritarianism, the stockpiling of guns and ammunition, or attacks on those scapegoated for the current state of desperation. Or one's fear about end times may manifest as an unhealthy obsession with apocalyptic fiction and conspiracy theories.

In any case, solid exegesis of the biblical text can help counter alarmism and provide a remedying dose of historical context. What we learn from Sumney's exegesis is that this text was not intended to stoke apocalyptic panic, but actually quell it by keeping a broader perspective on what is happening. Just as the Roman War in the first century was not a portent of the second coming of Jesus, neither are the calamitous events of our own time necessarily pointing to Jesus "coming in the clouds."

Preaching faithful alertness

If we understand that "there are no events in world history one can point to as clear evidence that the End is near," as Sumney notes above, what is the point of Jesus giving such dire warnings about the end times? If it doesn't mean building underground shelters stocked with canned peaches, or going into the woods with guns to train for taking out our enemies, what does it mean? What we learn—and what we must convey in our sermons—is that a more important focus is to live a life of *faithful alertness*.

The preacher can develop this idea of faithful alertness by discussing the two parables in this passage about the fig tree and the household keeping awake. Just as Jesus points to the fig tree, an illustration from nature, the sermon can also draw on images from Creation to illustrate the ways in which nature conveys important information—if we only pay attention. Congregations whose members live close to the land, water, and other elements of nature will understand this intuitively. Those whose connections to nature are more tenuous, or who live in settings where they are not as exposed to the rhythms of nature, will need robust descriptions to help the images come alive. In either case, it's worth noting that nature becomes Jesus' teaching partner; likewise, preachers can draw on nature in their own sermons.

The preacher can also offer a contemporary illustration of the parable of the household servants awaiting their master's return. What are examples of expectant waiting that will resonate with your congregation? You might tell two contrasting stories—one of "falling asleep" and being caught unprepared; and one of "keeping awake," alert to the signs of Jesus' imminent return. In this way, the preacher might employ a more realized eschatology to help the congregation prepare for Christ's appearance in the here and now, even as his ultimate arrival has not yet been fulfilled.

Mark 13:24–37

"GATHERING UP THE FRAGMENTS"

A Sermon on Mark 13:24–37; Isaiah 64:19

Leah D. Schade

(This sermon was preached at United in Christ Lutheran Church in Lewisburg, Pennsylvania, in 2011. The church stands atop a hill overlooking farmers' fields, and the congregation is made up of people who work the land, labor in factories, and have deep roots going back generations. Notice how the Scripture is contextualized for this particular congregation. Think about how you might take the images in this sermon around fragments and brokenness and apply them to your own preaching context.)

Have you noticed? There is a touch of melancholy in the late fall wind. It is a sad time of year.

I first felt this sadness a few weeks ago as I walked through the yard and kicked through the leaves blowing across the browning grass. Scattered fragments of the grand green trees of summer. Now I drive past the farmers' fields that had been verdant and thriving for so many months, producing abundant harvests to feed the multitudes. But now the stalks, which had been so huge, full and green, are shriveled, small and brown, draping limply to the cold ground.

"We all fade like a leaf," says Isaiah, "and our iniquities, like the wind, take us away" (Isa 64:6b).

Oh, we try to not to worry. We try not to feel that melancholy. We try to drown it out with Christmas carols played round the clock from the day after Halloween straight through to the end of the year. We try to shine the holiday lights into it and dispel the sadness. We try to ignore the gathering darkness as we crowd into the malls and stores, hoping we can buy our way out of it. But the melancholy descends on us as surely as the darkness of the winter solstice envelopes our ever-shortening days.

It is no wonder we feel a touch of anxiety, especially in light of this past year that our country and our world have endured. Natural disasters hit from all sides, with hurricanes, earthquakes, and floods of epic proportions. Political upheaval, war, and violent conflict continue to ravage countries and regions around the globe. Poverty of unprecedented proportions decimates entire populations of people. And pandemics of diseases gnaw away at our sense of security.

It's enough to make you feel as if we're living in the end times that Jesus alluded to in the Gospel of Mark: "In those days, after that suffering, the sun will be darkened, and the moon will not give its light, and the stars will be falling from heaven, and the powers in the heavens will be shaken" (13:24–25).

Biblical scholars date Mark's gospel either just before or just after the fall of the temple in Jerusalem. Mark was written sometime just before or just after the fall of the temple in Jerusalem, probably forty years after Jesus' death and resurrection. Mark was writing to a group of Christians who were wrestling with existential questions in light of this traumatic event. Is God not powerful after all? Has God rejected us? Does God not care about this sacred space that had been dedicated to worshiping God?

As I stand looking at the remnants of our fields and gardens, it causes me to wonder about this passage from Mark. What happens after the suffering? After the sun goes dark? After the moon fades away and the stars fall? After the tremors of the heavens die down?

What happens to all those broken pieces of people's lives? What happens to all the torn and tattered shreds of the messes we have made? As the author Flora Slosson Wuellner puts it: "What does God do with the useless leftovers of the universe, the unwanted, unlovely brokenness . . . ?"[4]

Jesus offers an answer in Mark 13:27: "Then he will send out the angels, and gather his elect from the four winds, from the ends of the earth to the ends of heaven."

Here is the key word: *gather*. God will gather up the fragments. And once they are gathered, God will transform them into something new and beautiful. Something we would never have thought could come from such a motley assembly of brokenness.

As I stood in my yard contemplating this thought, I realized that it was as near to me as the cycle of life going on all around me. Because Jesus goes on to say this: "From the fig tree learn its lesson: as its branch becomes tender and puts forth its leaves, you know that summer is near. So also, when you see these things taking place, you know that God is near, at the very gates" (13:28–29).

All these fallen leaves that I mourn will eventually become part of the soil and nutrients that feed the very tree from which they fell. All the

---

4. Wuellner, "A Broken Piece of Barley Bread," 7.

broken pieces will be gathered and reassembled into something new and creative.

God is here, even in this troubled time, preparing to gather the pieces together, just as God was with the people who originally heard these words. In Mark's community, they were dealing with their own trauma—the destruction of the temple in Jerusalem. This was the site where these Christians worshiped God. It was the most sacred of buildings where God made Godself present on earth. To see it overrun and destroyed by Roman soldiers brought everything they believed into question.

But Jesus' words are meant to tell the hard truth so that we can receive a startling revelation. God is not contained only in sacred buildings made by human hands. God's power transcends even the temple. And so we need not succumb to devastation when our temples fall. Because God is doing a new thing, bringing to us a future made up of these broken pieces.

This is good news for us who are the fragments of this world. Wuellner writes:

> What better [message of hope] for our throw-away abandoned people, our broken, fragmented humanity; our own individual shattered dreams, hopes, trust; all the shards of lives which have never been realized or fulfilled in wholeness . . .The core of Jesus' mission, more profound than even healing and restoration, is transformation . . . When re-formed by God's hands [the world and we] are fulfilled and empowered in a way we had never thought possible.[5]

This is why Jesus' words are so important, because they help us understand what to do as we're waiting for the fulfillment and the power to come from God. We are to remain alert, keep our eyes open and our minds attuned to catch glimpses of the God's work.

When we used to live in Philadelphia, my husband and I would go to a place called South Street and see an old, run-down building that someone had covered with a gorgeous mosaic of discarded glass and tile. I thought, what a powerful message in the heart of the city. "Listen, Philadelphians," it seemed to say, "there is no junk! You need only take the time to gather the pieces together and open your eyes to the vision that God wants you to see."

Or think of the quilts that our sewing group makes. They're made up of discarded pieces of fabric that fell away from the cutting table, faded after years of use, outgrown like yesterday's dresses. But like the mosaic on the

---

5. Wuellner, "A Broken Piece of Barley Bread," 8, 9.

side of that building, with the right vision these fragments can be gathered together and transformed into something that gives comfort and beauty as a quilted blanket for a baby or someone in need.

No fragment is worthless in God's eyes. Like the patches of cloth in this colorful quilt; like the side of this building on South Street covered in a mosaic of broken pieces, transforming the ugliness of this city block into a glimmering rainbow of artistic wonder—God will gather up even you and form you into the beautiful mosaic of the kingdom.

This is a life-giving message for us to hear on this first Sunday of Advent. Wedged between the holidays of Thanksgiving and Christmas, this is one of those awkward Sundays that we're not quite sure what to do with. It is a fragment, a leaf fallen between the cracks. It's a low-attendance Sunday. It's a Sunday that reminds us of all that is broken and fragmented in this world.

It's a Sunday when we stand in our empty gardens and fields, remembering All Saints Sunday in the not-too-distant past, the empty places at our holiday tables where our loved ones once laughed and ate with us. It's a Sunday that reminds us of what and who we have lost as well as the losses that are still to come.

But a parishioner of mine named Wanda once reminded me that there is a particular point in the liturgy that brings the memory of those saints into the very presence of God within our worship. It is the introduction to the Sanctus when the pastor concludes with these words: "And so with the hosts of heaven, we praise your name and join their unending hymn."

Wanda wrote me a letter in which she said, "I like to make sure that people understand the significance of that phrase. At this particular point in the liturgy my mind recalls family members who have died. Each Sunday it is a time when there is a feeling of closeness to those I knew and loved and especially those I shared communion with. They are now the hosts of heaven."[6]

This part of the liturgy is a reminder that we shared our life and our faith and that we still share our life and faith as we join in singing, "Holy, Holy, Holy." And in those moments that follow, there is no gap that separates us from those who have gone ahead. That is a part of the mystery of the Eucharist—in and through and with and under.

Wanda's letter reminds me that God gives us a tangible sign of this fragment-gathering, right here at the communion table, even as we are

---

6. Personal correspondence from E. Wanda Quay, October 28, 2005.

Mark 13:24-37

facing endings and brokenness. Each one of us is like a fragment of Christ's broken body. But when we share in this meal, we are rejoined and transformed into something even more miraculous and beautiful. Receiving communion is like being wrapped up in one of those quilts that our sewing group makes. Or being placed into a beautiful mosaic high on a building overlooking the city.

So as we stand in our own darkened gardens, blown by the chilly, melancholy wind, we remember that God stands with us. God is surveying the landscape, looking for every fragment that might be gathered and transformed, like fallen leaves forming the soil for tomorrow's grand green trees. Like broken pieces of tile and glass reworked into a magnificent piece of art on a dirty city building. Like discarded swatches of fabric sewn into a beautiful, warm quilt.

> . . .everything that is hurt, everything
> that seemed to us dark, harsh, shameful,
> maimed, ugly, irreparably damaged,
> is in [God] transformed
> and recognized as whole, as lovely,
> and radiant in [God's] light
> we awaken as the Beloved in every last part of our body.[7]

That was a poem written by the theologian Symeon the New Theologian, who lived at the turn of the first millennium. It captures the hope that we cling to in this first Sunday of Advent. As you receive communion, remember that you, too, are lovely and radiant in God's light. All the broken pieces, all the broken people, even the brokenness of Earth itself—all of it is beautiful in God's sight.

At this table, we remember that all of us are being gathered and transformed by God. Awaken as the Beloved in every last part of your body. Amen.

---

7. Symeon (949–1022 CE), *The Enlightened Heart*, 38–39.

Chapter 5

Matthew 24:36–44

(Year A—Advent—First Sunday of Advent)

³⁶"But about that day and hour no one knows, neither the angels of heaven, nor the Son, but only the Father. ³⁷For as the days of Noah were, so will be the coming of the Son of Man. ³⁸For as in those days before the flood they were eating and drinking, marrying and giving in marriage, until the day Noah entered the ark, ³⁹and they knew nothing until the flood came and swept them all away, so too will be the coming of the Son of Man. ⁴⁰Then two will be in the field; one will be taken and one will be left. ⁴¹Two women will be grinding meal together; one will be taken and one will be left. ⁴²Keep awake therefore, for you do not know on what day your Lord is coming. ⁴³But understand this: if the owner of the house had known in what part of the night the thief was coming, he would have stayed awake and would not have let his house be broken into. ⁴⁴Therefore you also must be ready, for the Son of Man is coming at an unexpected hour."

AN EXEGESIS OF MATTHEW 24:36–44

Jerry L. Sumney

Matthew 24:36–44 is a part of Matthew's expansion of the same discourse found in Mark 13. Jesus has left the temple for the last time (see chapter

4 above). On the way out, the disciples have commented that the temple is made of enormous stones, to which Jesus responds by saying that they will all be torn down. When Jesus and the disciples are alone, they ask him about the fall of the temple and the coming of the final judgment. Jesus then explains that the events that include the destruction of the temple (70 CE) are not signs that the end is near. All three Synoptic Gospels have this part of the story. We dealt with Mark first, because it was the first of the Gospels to be written. Matthew and Luke each read Mark's account of this discourse before they wrote theirs. So we can see the distinctive points they wanted to make as they expand Mark's version of the story.

Matthew adds our section and four long parables to Mark's account. All of this material except the final parable (25:31–46) is addressed to the church. The whole of this address to the church is about the delay of the second coming. Our reading serves as the introduction to the parables that follow it in chapters 24–25. Many of these parables end up dividing the characters into two groups, the saved and the not saved. To get the full import of this we have to keep in mind that both the saved and the not saved in these parables are members of the church. It becomes clear that for Matthew, being in the church is not enough to be saved.

All of this discussion of the end time emphasizes that no one can predict when the end will come. Matthew adds to Mark's first description of the coming of the Son of Man that all the peoples of the earth will see him and mourn. This helps him emphasize the open and worldwide nature of Christ's coming. Then, like Mark, he has Jesus tell the parable of the fig tree.

The first verse of our reading emphatically makes the point that no one knows when the end will come and no one knows the signs by saying that not even "the Son" knows when it will happen, but only God (Mark also has this saying, but Luke leaves it out.). The Son is clearly Jesus as he speaks. Identifying Jesus as the Son reminds readers of his exalted place with God. But at the same time, it places a limit on how he is related to God. God knows things that Christ does not. This seems to limit what we might think of as the divinity of Christ. But Matthew is not worried about that. His point is that *no one* can know when the end is coming. If the very Son of God does not know, there is no prediction from a mere human you should listen to.

This strong statement follows Matthew having Jesus say that the end will come "in this generation" (vv. 34–35). This seemingly threatening assertion tells readers they must always be prepared because the end is near.

But v. 36 puts this nearness in doubt because Jesus says he does not know when it will come. Including the assertion that it will happen in this generation seems strange. After all, Matthew is written after the generation Jesus is talking to is already past. Still, Matthew includes it. While Matthew probably thinks the end is near, it is clear that speculation about its timing is useless. What is really important is the certainty of its coming.

As we noted in connection with Mark 13, the church shifted quite quickly from accentuating the nearness of the second coming to talking about its certainty. Knowing that what God wants for the world will certainly come to pass is more important than knowing just when it will happen. Our whole reading wants to make it clear that not being able to predict the timing of the end does not affect its certainty.

The first image Matthew uses to talk about the impossibility of predicting the timing is that of the people who lived when Noah built the ark. They were going about their business as usual, doing the things people always do in the normal course of their lives. Then suddenly the flood comes and kills them. The only people who survived were those in the ark, those who were prepared for the cataclysm. When other Jewish writers of Matthew's time mention the people in Noah's time, they stress their wickedness. But that does not appear in Matthew. He wants the focus to be on them being unprepared for what they could not predict.

Matthew's second way to underscore the unpredictable nature of the second coming while saying you must always be prepared is to have two people doing the same thing in the normal course of life, and one is saved and one is not. He has two men working in a field, doing the same work. There does not seem to be any differences between them, but one is taken and one is not. Then he has two women working at a mill doing the same work and we hear of no difference between them, but one is taken and one is left. Matthew does not say why one is chosen over the other, but that will become clear in the short parable that follows and then yet more clear in the longer parables in chapters 24—25.

This image of some being taken and some being left has been used to impose the idea of a Rapture onto Matthew. But throughout Matthew, there is only one coming of the Son of Man. The being taken and being left are images of simultaneous judgment. Some are saved and some are condemned. In this image the people taken are parallel to those in the ark. They are separated and saved from those who remained. Being left here means they are excluded from those who are saved. Already in this discourse

Matthew 24:36–44

Matthew has had Jesus say that at the last day the Son of Man would send angels to gather the saved and bring them to him (24:30–31). Those who are left are those who will not get to participate in end time salvation; they suffer the final separation from God. In Matthew, the people of God are not removed from tribulations because he is describing the end of the world as we know it. This is Judgment Day. In Matthew, believers are not saved from sufferings and tribulations but are rather called to endure them faithfully.

The exhortation that flows from the unexpected taking up of one person but not the other is, "Be awake," or "Be alert" (v. 42). The unexpected and sudden nature of the coming does not call for speculation about when it will be, but for being ready for its coming all the time. Some interpreters think that the questions Matthew's church has about the second coming stem from more than being discouraged about how long it is taking. Since Matthew was written near the end of the first century, it may be that his church has faced some of the same retorts as the readers of 2 Peter 3:3–4. The church 2 Peter addresses seems to have some outsiders who are chiding them about the delay, saying it means that Christ's return will never happen. Or it may be that Matthew's church is both wondering why God does not put a swift end to their persecution and their facing of detractors who say they are silly to look for such an event. In either case, Matthew is warning his church not to doubt that the judgment is coming, even if it is taking longer than expected to arrive.

Our section ends with a short parable that draws on a widely used simile that says the end will come like a thief. That simile is expanded into a parable here that says if you knew when a thief was coming you would stop the break-in. But since you don't, you must be vigilant all the time. This parable is followed by another exhortation to be ready, because you cannot know when Christ will return.

The parables in the rest of chapter 24 and chapter 25 that our reading introduces all divide the characters into two groups: faithful and unfaithful servants, wise and foolish maidens. In each the rewarded people are those who are prepared for the coming but delayed event. Being prepared usually means they have done the job they were assigned. For the church this indicates that being prepared means they are living as God calls them to live. They are doing the good works God expects them to do. Matthew does not define those good works in these parables that address what church members should do. But the final parable of this set in 25:31–46 has Jesus talk about how non-believers will be evaluated, how "the nations" (or the

Gentiles) will be judged. The final fate of these non-believers is determined by how they responded to the physical needs of church members who were being persecuted.

Since taking care of the needs of those suffering is what God requires of non-believers, we can be sure that God expects nothing less from those in the church. The good deeds required include working to alleviate the pain of those who are suffering. Of course, it also includes all the other aspects of being a disciple that Jesus has spoken about throughout this Gospel.

More broadly we may say that being ready means living out your faith as one of the people of God who knows what God wants for God's world. God wants the social, economic, and political systems to reflect God's own goodness, love, and justice. God wants life within the church to be the example of what it looks like to structure a community based on who we know God to be in Christ. Again, a call to be ready for God's final and decisive act to claim God's own and God's world cannot lead to being passive as we wait for God to do something. For Matthew, remembering that Christ could return at any moment means that church members must be doing the good works God has set before them. Failure to be engaged in this work excludes you from participation in the salvation Christ is bringing.

We do not usually live with the expectation that Christ will come at any moment. If we were not in church and we were asked when the earth is going to end, we would answer with something like, "when the sun burns out," or "when we blow each other up." But we do not need to be looking to the sky for a trumpet to sound for this text to be important. Matthew knew that it is impossible to plot the timing of the end, but he proclaims that this does not make its coming less certain. This text is a promise that God will act to do justice for the faithful and the wicked. It should remind us of the certainty of the coming evaluation of our lives that we will receive from God. Matthew says we prepare for that coming judgment by being engaged in doing good works. He says that only those who prepare in this way will be given the blessed life with God.

Matthew 24:36–44

IDEAS FOR PREACHING ON MATTHEW 24:36-44

Leah D. Schade

Connecting Noah's story with the climate crisis

In his exegesis, Sumney notes that "[w]hile Matthew probably thinks the end is near, it is clear that speculation about its timing is useless. What is really important is the certainty of its coming." For Matthew, referencing the well-known story of Noah's building of the ark underscores this point. While the crowds mocked Noah's efforts, and while Noah could not give them an exact timetable for the coming of the flood, the fact that it was coming was still certain. The point Matthew has Jesus emphasize in this passage is that being prepared for that which we cannot predict is the key for the church. The same is as true for the church today as it was in Matthew's time.

Today's Christians may find Noah's story, as well as Jesus' warnings, to be similar to warnings we hear about what our world is facing with climate change. Certainly, there are important differences between the biblical apocalypse and the growing climate crisis. However, the points of correlation are eerily similar. While climate scientists cannot predict exactly what will happen or when, the apocalyptic scenarios are of frighteningly biblical proportions. David Wallace-Wells's book, *The Uninhabitable Earth: Life After Warming,* describes in explicit terms what human society will face when it comes to damage to our planet, including crop failures, increases in heat deaths, wars over resources, a surge of climate refugees, exotic diseases, unbreathable air, oceans unable to sustain life, and economic collapse.[1]

For both Matthew's readers and today's congregations, the call for being prepared is applicable in both cases. The preacher can help their congregation think about what preparation for the climate crisis might look like in their context. Does it mean outfitting the church building to temporarily house victims of catastrophic storms? Might it include installing solar panels to help mitigate carbon emissions? Or joining forces with the advocacy arm of the denomination to meet with legislators calling for climate action? A question for the preacher is: what is the role of the church

---

1. Wallace-Wells, *The Uninhabitable Earth.*

in the face of the climate crisis? How can we help prepare congregations and communities as part of our mission to the world?

The church as the ark

A sermon on Matthew 24:36–44 can also explore the image of the church as a kind of ark offering safety to those who are seeking refuge during apocalyptic times. Whether for refugees from other countries seeking asylum, or victims of domestic abuse in need of counseling and financial support, or LGBTQIA teens looking for a safe place to gather for fellowship, there are numerous opportunities for the church to serve as an ark for those in the midst of stormy seas.

Christian writers from Cyprian to Augustine to Luther to Calvin compared the church to Noah's ark, noting that the church should be a place of refuge, safety, and salvation. Frederick Buechner, too, picked up on the metaphor of the church as Noah's ark, which he describes in his book, *Beyond Words: Daily Readings in the ABC's of Faith*:

> In one as in the other, just about everything imaginable is aboard, the clean and the unclean both. They are all piled in together helter-skelter, the predators and the prey, the wild and the tame, the sleek and beautiful ones and the ones that are ugly as sin. There are sly young foxes and impossible old cows. There are the catty and the piggish and the peacock-proud. There are hawks and there are doves. Some are wise as owls, some silly as geese; some meek as lambs and others fire-breathing dragons. There are times when they all cackle and grunt and roar and sing together, and there are times when you could hear a pin drop. Most of them have no clear idea just where they're supposed to be heading or how they're supposed to get there or what they'll find if and when they finally do, but they figure the people in charge must know and in the meanwhile sit back on their haunches and try to enjoy the ride.[2]

Buechner points out that, of course, the ark is no joyride. "But even at its worst, there's at least one thing that makes it bearable within, and that is the storm without—the wild winds and terrible waves and in all the watery waste no help in sight."[3]

---

2. Buechner, *Beyond Words*, 277.
3. Buechner, *Beyond Words*, 277.

Matthew 24:36–44

What keeps the ship afloat and the inhabitants from harming each other is a certain trust that even in the midst of the watery blasts, there will be peace at the last and safe harbor in which to rest. The preacher can remind the congregation that part of what it means to be the church in times of upheaval such as what Matthew's congregation faced, is to provide shelter in the midst of turbulent times. That they can cling to each other and their faith in God is what can help to sustain them.

Apocalypse When?

"NOAH'S ARK AND CLIMATE CHANGE: WHAT KIND OF CHURCH WILL WE BE?"

A Sermon on Genesis 6:5–13, 9:8–17 and Matthew 24:36–44

Leah D. Schade

(This is a sermon I have preached at various churches and conferences addressing the climate crisis. Note that Matthew did not place the emphasis on the Noah story in the way I am using it for this sermon. Matthew has Jesus referring to Noah merely to illustrate the unexpected nature of return of the Son of Man. In this sermon, however, I am emphasizing the story of Noah for the way it parallels what we are facing with the climate crisis. Nevertheless, the theme of being prepared in the face of imminent upheaval and watching for Christ's return all the while is the message both of this sermon and the pericope in Matthew.)

The story of Noah's ark is iconic. When I was among the new-parent set, I remember shopping for baby items for my children and seeing cute renditions of the ark with adorable giraffes, hippos, and horsies poking their heads out of the windows and smiling from the deck. Kids love the image of all the animals floating together in a big sea-going zoo.

But in this passage from Matthew, Jesus is not thinking about cute animals and a smiling dove. My guess is that he might have had in mind an image closer to the 2014 Darren Aronofsky film *Noah*. The movie portrays the tragedy of the cataclysmic destruction of life on Earth. Frankly, the thought of it is overwhelming. And despite our efforts to soften the story, children can still grasp the enormity of the loss. I remember talking about Noah's Ark in a children's sermon once, and one child asked, "What happened to all the other animals who weren't on the ark? And the people?" Er, uh . . .

We rush to the iconic dove and the rainbow—God's promise to never again destroy the Earth. But the truth is, the planet suffered immense loss in that primordial flood.

Here's the truth, child. When human beings fill the earth with violence, everyone suffers. Even the animals. When human hearts are corrupt and filled with evil, the consequences for the innocent are unbearable (Gen 6:5–13). Yes, the animals died. Yes, the people died. And it's okay to be sad about that. Because it's not fair, and it's not right.

Today we are living in what will become a future generation's mythic saga of our planetary catastrophe. And our children are already cognizant of this dystopian future. In fact, they are keenly aware of what lies ahead for them. At Thanksgiving dinner a few years ago, our family was talking about world events and politics when my then–eleven-year-old daughter piped up, "I don't know why you're talking about all this. None of it is going to matter. The apocalypse is already happening. The end of the world is coming."

Forks clattered. Mouths stood agape with half-swallowed mashed potatoes. All eyes turned to me, the ecofeminist–climate activist mom. I shrunk in my chair. I never actually used the word *apocalypse* when explaining climate change to her. How did she come up with that?

"Why are you looking at her?" my daughter asked. "Don't you read the news? It's not her fault. She's just trying to warn us."

Did God try to warn others before speaking to Noah?

Had others been given the divine warning about the impending global disaster and refused to heed the call to prepare? By the same token, did people mock Jesus' warnings about being prepared for the coming of the Son of Man? Did they dismiss him? Did Matthew's readers write him off?

We know Noah's urgent pleas to his neighbors were laughed off as the crazy doomsday scare tactics of a lunatic. In the same way, the warnings of climate scientists today are often dismissed, ridiculed, mocked, and silenced. They are not giving up, of course. But with an all-out assault on the climate and environmental protections by the most powerful nation on Earth, the window of opportunity seems to be narrowing even further.

Of course, the logistics of getting all those species on a single seafaring vessel is quite absurd and impossible. Just think about how many living creatures Noah would have had to collect and fit on that ark. Here's a list: "7000 species of worms; 50,000 species of arachnids; 900,000 species of insects; 2500 species of amphibians; 6000 species of reptiles; 8600 species of birds; and 3500 species of mammals; plus food for one and all."[4]

How big would that boat have to be? Here's the thing: "The only vessel truly capable of holding all these is Spaceship Earth."[5]

But this fragile planetary vessel floating in a sea of darkness and stars has once again been filled with violence. We are finding ourselves with

---

4. Walker, *The Woman's Dictionary of Symbols and Sacred Objects*, 85.
5. Walker, *The Woman's Dictionary of Symbols and Sacred Objects*, 85.

Noah in a Genesis 6 moment. Too many human hearts are corrupt and filled with evil, and the consequences for the innocent are unbearable.

Because it's not just the climate crisis that plagues this Earth. It is a convergence of global crises swirling into a perfect storm on the horizon. The cost of our primary source of energy—fossil fuels—is poisoning water, land, sky, and bodies. The explosion of the human population is about to reach unsustainable levels. Financial crises have swept across our human society. And, yes, ecological issues regarding water supplies, global warming, garbage, and pollution are threatening the health of the planet itself.

Add to this the accompanying threats of terrorism and war as a result of these conflicts over land and resources (and exacerbated by climate change) and we are, once again, facing a flood of catastrophic proportions. A flood of people, a flood of poverty, a flood of violence, and yes, the actual flooding of the coastlands and river around the world.

But this time the flood is not coming from God. It's coming from humankind.

It's hard not to see Noah's story as a future-present allegory for our own time. In Genesis, God promised to never again destroy the Earth (Gen 9:8–17). But human beings apparently are not willing to make that same promise. When we put country over planet, when we value our current comfort over our children's survival, it appears some fatal genetic flaw was passed to us from Adam and Eve through Noah. He and his family were, after all, descendants of the first humans who took what they wanted, despite divine warnings of dire consequences.

What does this mean for us? And what are the implications for the church called by Jesus to prepare for what is to come? It means we must live out our faith as the people of God for this time and place facing these unique challenges. It means working for the kind of world God wants for us, even when we have gone so far in the wrong direction and we fear there is no return.

In her book *Living Beyond the End of the World*, Margaret Swedish minces no words:

> Nothing will make this wrenching transition go away; we can neither avoid it nor escape it. We have nowhere to go. We will either find a way to live through it, with dignity, with integrity, with hope (not optimism), or we will go through it with mounting human suffering . . . We are coming to the end of the world, or at least to the end of a world. How it ends will be very much up to us. We

Matthew 24:36–44

have many choices in front of us, but not this one—that the world we know is ending.[6]

There will be drastic changes in how we live and what we do to survive. And for many people, it *will* be a matter of survival. In fact, for a large portion of the world's people, it already is a question of basic survival.

This means that Christians have an opportunity—and an obligation—to talk about how we can respond to the climate crisis. Just as the ark of old was a place of refuge, the church, too, needs to be a place of safety and security for those who are affected by climate change. The church must serve as a kind of "ark," not just for humanity, but for all Creation. Comparisons of the church to Noah's Ark have been made since the very beginning of the church. It makes sense for Christians to advocate for all species of plants and animals, as well as the most vulnerable human communities, to find refuge on this ark of planet Earth.

Thankfully, more and more followers of Jesus and other faith communities are making Creation care a priority. An increasing number of religious groups are working to create healthy and safe communities for our families as they come to view ecological issues as a matter of living out the Golden Rule. Nine different denominations have moved to divest from fossil fuels. There are also ecumenical and interfaith organizations that are advocating for protecting God's Creation, such as Interfaith Power & Light, eco-America's Blessed Tomorrow, GreenFaith, and the Poor People's Campaign.

In terms of more immediate danger, many houses of worship are preparing now for climate-related disasters when they happen. They are following Jesus call to "keep awake," to stay alert for opportunities to minister in the midst of crisis. My own Lutheran denomination (ELCA), for example, has an entire division called Lutheran Disaster Response (LDR). What's great about LDR is that not only do they arrive on the scene when disasters hit, but they stay with communities long after the media spotlight has moved on. They remain committed to the people and neighborhoods in need of help until they have restored their lives and communities. As we're seeing increasing numbers of climate-exacerbated weather catastrophes, LDR and other church emergency agencies will be needed more and more.

The ark of the Church must be there to assist people, restore some sense of sanity, provide aid and relief, and help to rebuild. We've seen that happen over and over again, whether they are victims of hurricanes, droughts,

---

6. Swedish, *Living Beyond the "End of the World,"* 156, 158.

floods, or wildfires. The ark of the Church is there for them, sending forth the dove of peace, and pointing to the rainbow overhead promising God's ever-present care.

But people of faith must also add their voices and votes to the calls for immediate changes in our energy policies, meat consumption, carbon-burning lifestyles, and industries that are causing the flood of injustice and poverty to rise at unprecedented rates. Faith leaders in wealthy countries need to model moral responsibility and stewardship that constrains consumption and restores balance with the ecological systems that support human life. Margaret Swedish describes the challenge this way:

> What is required now, and this must be the content of the call, is that this nation and other rich countries—and our religious and pastoral leaders as well—be summoned to turn toward a new way of life, one that puts our consumption and waste back into balance with nature, into a relationship with the earth that allows the earth to heal, restore, regenerate what is needed to continue the story of life, while at the same time making it possible for poor people to no longer be poor . . . This will be the hardest thing we have ever done.[7]

However, we must do it. And we can do it.

We're in the hot, crowded ark. The flood waters are rising. We must ask ourselves: What kind of church will we be? What kind of person is Jesus calling me to be?

As I remind my children every time we see a rainbow: God has promised to be with us, no matter what we face, and even if it is by our own hand. That promise is refracted by millions upon millions of tiny prism droplets in the sky, forming the colors of the rainbow that fill us with hope.

---

7. Swedish, *Living Beyond the "End of the World,"* 171.

Chapter 6

Luke 21:25–36

(Year C—Advent—First Sunday in Advent)

^{25} "There will be signs in the sun, the moon, and the stars, and on the earth distress among nations confused by the roaring of the sea and the waves. ^{26}People will faint from fear and foreboding of what is coming upon the world, for the powers of the heavens will be shaken. ^{27}Then they will see 'the Son of Man coming in a cloud' with power and great glory. ^{28}Now when these things begin to take place, stand up and raise your heads, because your redemption is drawing near." ^{29} Then he told them a parable: "Look at the fig tree and all the trees; ^{30}as soon as they sprout leaves you can see for yourselves and know that summer is already near. ^{31}So also, when you see these things taking place, you know that the kingdom of God is near. ^{32}Truly I tell you, this generation will not pass away until all things have taken place. ^{33}Heaven and earth will pass away, but my words will not pass away. ^{34} Be on guard so that your hearts are not weighed down with dissipation and drunkenness and the worries of this life, and that day does not catch you unexpectedly, ^{35}like a trap. For it will come upon all who live on the face of the whole earth. ^{36}Be alert at all times, praying that you may have the strength to escape all these things that will take place, and to stand before the Son of Man."

Apocalypse When?
An Exegesis of Luke 21:25–36

Jerry L. Sumney

This is the third reading from the Synoptic Apocalypse that we are treating in this book. While there is a good deal of overlap in the three lections that come from it, there are also distinctive features that warrant our attention. All three share that they are written to churches that have experienced persecution. This discourse of Jesus assures them that their persecution does not mean they have displeased God. Instead, it says persecution is what the faithful should expect as the powers of evil oppose God's will.

Matthew and Luke write to churches who know the temple has fallen. Even if the temple has not yet been razed, Mark's church knows that it will be because Rome has laid siege to Jerusalem. Like Mark, Luke's church has mostly Gentile members. As we noted in connection with Mark 13, the fall of the temple is difficult for them even though they were not Jewish. They had committed themselves to worshiping only the God of Israel but now that God's only temple has been destroyed. They have to ask what that means about the God they are worshiping. Does it mean this God is not powerful enough to defend that one temple? This discourse of Jesus assures them that he knew of the temple's destruction and he says it is less important than it might seem. Specifically, he says that it is not a sign of the end. For Luke's readers this may be a needed assurance because the temple's fall may have happened two decades earlier. If some had interpreted it as a sign that the end was near, the delay might lead some to give up hope that God would act to reclaim the world and vindicate the persecuted.

The churches of all three Synoptic Gospels, of course, have questions about the delay of the second coming. The earliest church saw the resurrection of Jesus as the beginning of the resurrection of all people and the coming of the Judgment Day. But now decades have passed and the end has not come. They need help understanding what this delay means and help thinking about how they should live. In this discourse, Luke has Jesus help them frame their lives in the time between his resurrection and the second coming.

In all three of the Synoptics, this discourse is a part of some of the final words of Jesus. He has caused a disturbance in the temple courtyard and argued with those in charge of temple. Then as he leaves the temple for the last time, his disciples take note of the size and beauty of the temple. Jesus responds by telling them it will all be torn down. Once they are alone with Jesus, they ask him when that would happen and what signs there would be that it is coming. Jesus begins his response by telling the disciples not to pay attention to people who claim to be the messiah (Luke 21:8-11) and by warning them about coming persecution (Luke 21:12-19). Just before our text in Luke, Jesus describes the destruction of the temple (21:20-24).

Our reading begins with a description of cosmic upheavals. This imagery sets the coming of the Son of Man apart from the destruction of Jerusalem. This is not the first reference to these kinds of signs in this discourse. Already in 21:8-11 they were mentioned as things that would come after persecution, betrayal, and the fall of Jerusalem. Luke's description of these upheavals is more extensive than that in Mark but is similar to the expansion of this saying in Matthew 24:29-31. Both draw on imagery from the prophets. Luke draws the imagery of the signs in the sun, moon, and stars and the description of nations being distressed and people being afraid from Isaiah 8 and 13. These Isaiah texts describe a theophany, an appearance of God. Luke here suggests that the appearance of the "Son of Man" is a theophany. By now, all of Luke's readers know that Jesus is the Son of Man. So, in some measure, Luke assigns the coming Christ a divine role.

It is important to notice the different reactions to the appearance of Christ who comes in judgment. The nations are afraid and perplexed. People are even fainting from fear. But believers are to look up in hope and expectation; their salvation is arriving. The announcement of coming judgment is a threat to some because justice will be meted out. But it is a blessing to others, and for the same reason. In vv. 25-27, it is "they" who will be afraid. In v. 28, it is "you" who will be happy. Luke draws his readers into the group talked about in Jesus' promise. Whatever persecution they have endured and however tired they are of waiting, they are the faithful who will be pleased to see Christ returning with the power to set them free.

The metaphor of redemption is used here to describe the salvation Christ is bringing. "Redemption" (*apolytrōsis*) is the term used to speak of paying a ransom for a person who had been kidnapped or who was taken prisoner in a war. This image of salvation envisions believers being rescued from powers that have imprisoned them. The return of Christ means they are freed to live a new life with Christ. This image speaks powerfully to these readers who know persecution. Indeed, it speaks powerfully to all who are trapped in any kind of oppression or any situation they feel helpless to overcome. Freedom is the promise that the judgment of Christ brings.

Apocalypse When?

To make sure this promise of salvation does not lead to attempts to plot out the exact day that Christ will return, the Parable of the Fig Tree follows it. This parable intends to convey a general analogy rather than giving details that have allegorical meanings (like the Parable of the Sower is given allegorical meanings). This parable says that you can tell summer is near when you see the buds on the fig tree. Of course, by the time the fig tree buds, it is basically summer. So, seeing them has no predictive power at all. Jesus says that is the way it is with the second coming: by the time there are signs, it will already be here. You get no warning about its coming.

As in the other Gospels, Jesus says "all these things" will happen before "this generation" passes away (v. 32). This is troublesome for us because we know that the generation of the apostles died and Christ did not return. It would also have been troublesome for the original readers of these Gospels. We saw in our discussion of Mark 13 that Mark has Jesus turn to address the readers by saying, "What I say to you I say to everyone" (13:37). Thus, he makes each generation of readers the ones being addressed. Luke does not do that.

Interpreters have offered a number of ways to read this text. Some contend that Luke has in mind a few octogenarians who are of that generation who are still alive. Thus, he expects the end to be very soon, before those senior citizens die. Some think that we should just admit that Luke (and the other Evangelists) got it wrong. Others think "all these things" refers only to the fall of temple, not the immediately preceding verses. Still others contend that in Luke "this generation" does not designate a particular time frame. Rather, throughout his Gospel, Luke uses this expression for people who reject Jesus and refuse to accept that God is acting through him to bring salvation (see 7:31; 9:41; 11:29–33, 50–51; 16:8; 17:25).

The least likely of these interpretations is that Luke is thinking of really old people who are still alive from the generation of the apostles. That would lead readers to think that the end was very near and that there are signs of its coming—the death of those people. Whatever it means, it is not intended to increase speculation about the nearness of the end because that is what the Parable of the Fig Tree rejects. In addition, whatever Luke means must not count against the assurance of v. 33. That verse says that the promise of Christ's coming is certain. If Luke has the apostolic generation in mind, his readers know that it has passed. That would weaken the credibility of the promise that Christ's word will not pass away, that his promise of vindication is certain. But what Luke wants his readers to hear is that this promise is certain.

The promise that Christ will return supports the exhortations that conclude this discourse in Luke. Luke encourages his readers to be certain of that promise to give them courage not to let their hearts be weighed down, not to become discouraged (21:34). Luke says believers must always be ready for the coming of Christ, otherwise it will catch them like a trap. That is, they will be those people who are afraid rather than joyful. Luke here sees falling into an immoral life as evidence of becoming discouraged and so failing to be prepared for the coming Christ. Interestingly, he adds one other symptom of waning belief in coming blessing and judgment: being weighed down with the cares or worries of life. Failing to remember the justice and blessing that are the final state of all things can lead to losing one's perspective on things that are happening around them. Believers can reject the priorities and values of the world around them by remembering that God promises to make all things right. If they keep that reality in view it can help keep them from becoming discouraged. They can know that the evaluations of them and their beliefs that derive from the culture's values are false if they remember that it is the judgment of Christ that is true and ultimate. Luke wants his readers to evaluate all things in light of what God promises to do in Christ.

At the same time, this eschatological discourse has acknowledged that the path of faith is not easy. Jesus says the faithful will be persecuted and betrayed, they will endure the destruction of the temple, and they will be discouraged by the delay in Christ's return. So, the discourse ends by encouraging the readers to be ready always, to pray for strength to escape the troubles, and to be able to live a life that will be approved at judgment. Encouraging the readers to pray for these things suggests that they will not be left alone to accomplish them. While they await the second coming, God will be present with them, giving them hope and helping them live the life God wants for them.

Like other texts we have seen, the purpose of this discussion of the end times is to give hope and to encourage faithfulness. Luke has Jesus speak of his disciples as those who will be glad to see him return in judgment (v. 28). He also reminds the readers that they must remain faithful to be one of those happy people. Luke's warning about the worries of this life does not suggest that this talk of the end means believers should not care about the world around them. Luke spends much of his Gospel talking about God's care for people who are disadvantaged and about how God expects God's people to respond to those needs. Luke encourages readers so they can continue to work for the good of those around them by seeing that work through the promise of Christ's return, a return that will establish the justice God's people work for. That is the perspective that gives meaning and hope to doing God's will in the world.

Luke 21:25-36

IDEAS FOR PREACHING ON LUKE 21:25-36

Leah D. Schade

Contextualizing persecution

Most Christians in the United States will not have had direct experience with the kind of persecution experienced by the Lukan community. So the preacher will need to provide some historical background for what the early church faced and make comparisons to the types of persecution that Christians in contemporary contexts have endured. One way to do this is by pointing out that there are places in the world where Christians face the kind of ill treatment that the early church suffered. If the congregation supports overseas missions or sends missionaries to places where conditions are difficult or even dangerous, the sermon may be an ideal opportunity to highlight this ministry and its importance for the church at home and globally.

The preacher may even ask for a person doing this missionary work to share what it's like to be in that place. What conflicts do they see? What "famines" or "plagues" have they observed? In what ways have governments or other institutions of power hindered or even opposed the ministry of the church in that region?

The sermon will also need to lift up how God is sustaining the work of the church in these places. In response to these challenges, how has the missionary found ways to endure? In what ways have they experienced the power of Christ giving them the words they need and the strength that is necessary to persevere? In other words, what gives them hope when hope seems in short supply?

Is redemption good news or bad news?

Above, Sumney notes that Christ's appearance at the Parousia will be received differently depending on whether the hearers are insulated and comfortable or persecuted and oppressed. So the preacher will want to be sensitive to the ways their congregation may receive this text. For example, a church of mainly well-to-do, privileged individuals may need a prophetic warning that the things in which they find their comfort, success, and evidence of divine blessings will not last, just as the temple in Jerusalem did not. The sermon can ask what our "temples" might be today and why they inspire the kind of awe the disciples experienced. What are the physical or institutional structures that seem impervious but are, in fact, more fragile than their appearance suggests? Knowing that such structures cannot last, what might be the disciplines of spiritual and social justice that the congregation can undertake now so as to prepare themselves for Christ's coming?

On the other hand, for communities that labor under heavy burdens of racialization, colonization, economic oppression, environmental persecution, or political conflict, Jesus' words about upheaval can be, paradoxically, reassuring that this is inaugurating a new beginning of justice and an end to empire. Just as Luke's listeners needed reassurance to endure in order to "gain their souls," listeners will need assurance that their suffering is not without meaning, but is, in fact, an opportunity to experience the nearness of Christ in unexpected ways.

What does "redemption" look like?

Verse 28 of this passage calls upon believers to lift their heads in expectation because their redemption is coming. Sumney notes that the Greek word, *apolytrōsis*, refers to paying a ransom for someone who has been kidnapped or taken as a prisoner in a war. Since this image of salvation encourages believers to see Christ as one who rescues them from imprisonment, the preacher may want to explore the different ways in which powerful forces hold people in bondage.

For example, how have the opioid crisis or other addictions affected the community? Perhaps there are mental health issues that are shaking the foundations of families, schools, or the church. Or there may be soldiers returning from active duty who are dealing with issues such as PTSD, depression, or suicidal thoughts. If, as Sumney states, "the return of Christ means they are freed to live a new life with Christ," what will this redemption look like? And how might the church participate in this redemption? Leaning towards a more realized eschatology, the preacher can share stories of communities coming together to look at these underlying and intersecting issues in order to find solutions that bring the freedom that Christ promises.

Luke 21:25–36

"GAINING OUR SOULS"

A Sermon on Luke 21:25–36

Leah D. Schade

(This sermon was preached at St. Thomas Lutheran Church in Richmond, Kentucky, in the fall of 2019. It was a time of significant political upheaval in the country in which many congregations experienced divisiveness and their pastors sometimes hesitated to broach the moral and ethical issues surrounding the presidential administration of the day. In this sermon, I opted for a more "political" theme as it related to the persecution experienced by the Lukan church. I connected the situation of the early church to both the church in Nazi Germany as well as the church resisting the rise of authoritarianism in the present time.)

I recently read a book where I came across these words describing a certain leader and his rise to power: "He seems to have thought about how Christians would view him . . . He certainly did not hesitate to reference God and to suggest divine support of his [agenda] . . . Getting off on the right foot with Christians in [this country] was certainly an early priority."[1] Further on, the author writes: "Surely if we have learned anything at all about [this leader], it is that nothing he ever said could be taken at face value. We must test his every word against what actually took place. These pious words . . . have no basis in reality. [It] is just another example of propaganda."[2]

Can you guess who the author is talking about? The author is Dean Stroud and he is writing about Adolf Hitler. The book is called *Preaching in Hitler's Shadow: Sermons of Resistance in the Third Reich,* and it was written in 2013. His book is about the way Hitler used Christianity to give a patina of religious legitimacy to his Nazi ideology. The book includes thirteen sermons by pastors who saw what was happening and courageously spoke out against the Third Reich.

In the book's introduction, Stroud reminds readers of exactly how Hitler and the Nazis were different from the version of Christianity they put in place for Germany:

1. Stroud, *Preaching in Hitler's Shadow*, 45.
2. Stroud, *Preaching in Hitler's Shadow*, 5.

> Although the Nazi program included a counterfeit "positive Christianity" and although Hitler peppered speeches with references to God, neither he nor Nazism had a single thing in common with traditional Christianity. Nazi religion was pagan, containing a pagan savior and creed. The creed knew nothing of sin, and its faith glorified violence. Nazism had no meekness or humility, no love of neighbor, and no thought of forgiveness. Hitler was the German savior and Jews were the devil incarnate. Both Christianity and Nazism spoke of a Reich (empire, kingdom), but they had vastly different understandings about its meaning.[3]

Similarly, some national leaders today claim divine sanction for their actions. One country's leader has quoted an evangelical talk show host who said he was like "the King of Israel" and "the second coming of God."[4] This same leader also described himself as "the chosen one" while looking up at the sky.

Some religious leaders even claim divine power for themselves as they work their way into the halls of political power. A prosperity gospel minister by the name of Paula White has proclaimed that "wherever I go, God rules. When I walk on White House grounds, God walks on White House grounds ... because where I stand is holy."[5]

With all of this in the background, we hear these words from Jesus: "Beware that you are not led astray; for many will come in my name and say, 'I am he!' and, 'The time is near!' Do not go after them."

These words are from chapter 21 of Luke's gospel, and are part of Jesus' apocalyptic discourse. Scholars believe Luke was written in 85 CE, not long after the destruction of the temple in Jerusalem, and more than fifty years after Jesus' death and resurrection. What is disconcerting is that this section of the Gospel describes circumstances that seem to be happening today as well: "Nation will rise against nation, and kingdom against kingdom; there will be great earthquakes, and in various places famines and plagues; and there will be dreadful portents and great signs from heaven" (vv. 10–11). This sounds very much like what we're seeing around the world, doesn't it? So, does this mean we are living in the end times?

Fundamentalist Christians who want to sell us books like *The Late, Great Planet Earth*, or the *Left Behind* series, or the *Harbinger* series would like us to think so. Millennialist Christians in government who are angling

---

3. Stroud, *Preaching in Hitler's Shadow*, 9.
4. Bailey, "'I am the chosen one.'"
5. *Now This News*, "Trump's Faith Advisor Paula White Is Now a White House Staffer."

for war in the Middle East in order to hasten the second coming of Christ would like us to think so. But speculation about the end times and Christ's second coming is not what Jesus is advocating here. Rather, he is giving instructions to his disciples about what to expect whenever a despotic regime takes over, no matter where or when that happens. Because whether you support or resist the government leaders of our day, the fact is that every generation goes through periods where political, cultural, and societal pressures build up until they reach a crisis point. Then there are ruptures that tear at the fabric of civilization.

It appears that we are in the midst of one of these cycles. And it is precisely these kinds of conditions that create chaos in society. Chaos, in turn, breeds fear. Fear, for its part, drives people to follow men and women who seize power and who surround themselves with the trappings of religion in order to create an illusion of divine providence.

This is what happened during the Roman empire when Luke was writing this gospel. The Caesar was to be regarded as a god. It also happened in post-War World I Germany. With Hitler as the fuhrer, he and the German state were to be worshiped and given complete obedience. And there are indications that we are seeing this pattern repeat itself in authoritarian-dominated countries around the world today.

Jesus warned his listeners to be prepared for this pattern. He tells them not to be shocked when dictators arrest those who speak out against them and persecute those deemed to be enemies. Whether that takes the form of tweets and smear campaigns, or sending thugs to attack anti-corruption activists, or encouraging violence against journalists, or methodical, organized ethnic cleansing and genocide, we are not to be surprised when it happens. Yes, it is shocking. But we should not be caught off-guard like a deer in the headlights. And we are not to fall under the sway of mesmerizing or seemingly strong leaders who claim God's authority while they are, in fact, doing the exact opposite of what God has told us is right and just.

Further, we are not to doubt God when this chaos is happening. If the world is falling apart, we are not to see it as a sign of God's abandonment. Instead, Jesus says that "this will give you an opportunity to testify" (v. 13). In Greek, the word is *martyrion,* which means "to give a witness." This means that if you're a preacher—preach the gospel! If you are a lay person, use your words and actions in whatever spheres of influence in which you find yourself in order to live out the teachings of Jesus. Teachings like, love your neighbor, care for the least of these, forgive your enemies. In other words, everything that the corrupt leadership ignores, makes fun of, mocks, or even punishes—this is what Christians must do to maintain their moral clarity and their faith.

Jesus did recognize, however, that holding fast to his teachings may place you in opposition to everything and everyone you're supposed to hold in high regard. This can include your family, your boss, even your nation. How many of you have felt a rift with family members or friends in the last few years over the political state of our country? Some of you may even feel a rift with your fellow church members. Or you may feel that a sermon like this one is not appropriate because it's "too political" and contributes to the divisiveness we're experiencing. You would not be alone in thinking this.

I have taught, researched about, and talked with hundreds of pastors over the past three years. Many of them are stymied when some parishioners walk out of their sermons, send angry emails, confront them face to face, or threaten to withdraw their financial support, even when the sermon mentions nothing about the president or could in anyway be construed to be critiquing this administration.

This indicates that something much deeper is going on—something that involves the presence of a twisted theology that, when confronted with the actual teachings of Jesus, challenges and threatens a particular worldview in some way. This can lead to anger, mistrust, defensiveness, withdrawal, and even threats.

That's what the pastors in Germany faced when they spoke out against the Reich. They were told to keep their mouths shut and not to criticize what they saw happening in their country. If they disobeyed and preached the gospel anyway, many of them were removed from their churches. Some were put on trial or driven out of the country. A few were even executed.

Thankfully, US pastors have not yet faced this kind of backlash directly from the government. But the pressure from their parishioners to remain silent in the face of injustice is real and it takes many forms. What is it like for pastors to be preaching in an authoritarian shadow? Here is what some of them have said in surveys and interviews I've conducted.

> "I have lost members over the past two years due to preaching about race. There are only so many losses a small congregation can handle."
>
> "I have received threats in the past and worry that they might be acted upon if I continued to speak as freely as I would like."
>
> "One person threatened to disrupt a dialogue we were planning to have about the role of the church in a divided society. We

explained that this wasn't about trying to change people's political orientation. It was just about how to learn to listen to each other and share our experiences in order to find common values. But this person was just so angry that we would even consider having this conversation in the church. It was very unsettling."

Several pastors have also told me that they have been accused of having a "liberal agenda" for just preaching the values of the Bible such as welcoming the foreigner, showing kindness to strangers, being compassionate, and caring for God's Creation. All of this is seen as a thinly veiled critique of the president and his administration.

Interestingly, this is exactly what happened in Nazi Germany when the pastors refused to align with the Reich's ideology. "Every sermon that advocated basic Christian virtues challenged the Nazi way of being . . . As Christians know from the New Testament, especially the Acts of the Apostles, simply preaching the gospel in the face of evil is sufficient to provoke violent response."[6]

As Jesus said: "You will be betrayed even by parents and brothers, by relatives and friends; and they will put some of you to death. You will be hated by all because of my name. But not a hair of your head will perish. By your endurance you will gain your souls" (vv. 16–19).

What does this endurance look like?

For the pastor who decided to go ahead with the dialogue in their church, it took the form of patience and deep listening, allowing the parishioner to express their thoughts and work through their concerns. In the end, they discovered that they can, in fact, have these difficult conversations in a way that helps them identify not just what their differences are, but what they have in common. By their endurance they gained their souls.

Another pastor wrote in the questionnaire about their unique context serving a church inside the Washington DC beltway. "I'm preaching to policy-makers and political appointees who are incredibly well-informed. They're also tired of politics when they get to church and need inspiration to keep fighting the good fight. I want to bolster their faith to enable them to go into their workplaces and have courage to enact the gospel."

In other words, despite the risk, many pastors know that they are called by God, called by Jesus, and called by the church to preach the gospel—even when it runs counter to the prevailing attitudes of certain

---

6. Stroud, *Preaching in Hitler's Shadow*, 20.

leaders. As one pastor put it: "I receive negative pushback, and people have left. But I must preach gospel and it is political. Period."

Stroud notes that the courageous pastors in Nazi Germany viewed preaching as vitally important for providing a counter-message to the Reich. "Christian vocabulary, so different from the poisonous words of Nazi rhetoric, offered pastor and congregation a subversive language through which to share the faith and extend comfort."[7]

"Reading these sermons in the twenty-first century," Stroud says, "one cannot help but marvel at the confidence these preachers placed in the proclaimed word of God . . . The preacher expected concentration and attention. Even more, the preacher expected the courage of faith. Urgent as things might be outside the church, preaching the word of God was even more urgent inside the church."[8]

I'll leave you with one final thought written by a pastor who was the first to be murdered by the Nazis. His name was Paul Schneider, and this is what he wrote about preaching in Nazi Germany: "It is not that I and all the rest of us have said too much in our sermons, but rather that we have said far too little."[9]

Schneider was like Dietrich Bonhoeffer, a Lutheran pastor who also resisted the Reich and was killed by the Nazis. He believed so completely in the mercy, compassion, and justice of Jesus Christ, he was willing to preach the gospel at all costs. I have no doubt that by their endurance, they gained their souls.

We, too, as pastors and parishioners, as Christians who confess our faith in the crucified and resurrected Jesus, must continue to testify and to bear witness. We can do this trusting that Christ is with us and will give us the words. He will, in fact, give us the endurance we need. And by this endurance we *will* gain our souls. Amen.

---

7. Stroud, *Preaching in Hitler's Shadow*, 43.
8. Stroud, *Preaching in Hitler's Shadow*, 48.
9. Stroud, *Preaching in Hitler's Shadow*, 47.

Chapter 7

1 Corinthians 15:19–26

(Year C—Easter—Resurrection of the Lord)

> [19] *If for this life only we have hoped in Christ, we are of all people most to be pitied.* [20] *But in fact Christ has been raised from the dead, the first fruits of those who have died.* [21] *For since death came through a human being, the resurrection of the dead has also come through a human being;* [22] *for as all die in Adam, so all will be made alive in Christ.* [23] *But each in his own order: Christ the first fruits, then at his coming those who belong to Christ.* [24] *Then comes the end, when he hands over the kingdom to God the Father, after he has destroyed every ruler and every authority and power.* [25] *For he must reign until he has put all his enemies under his feet.* [26] *The last enemy to be destroyed is death.*

AN EXEGESIS OF 1 CORINTHIANS 15:19–26

Jerry L. Sumney

The Corinthian church seems to have been one of Paul's most problematic congregations. When he writes 1 Corinthians they have people who use their spiritual gifts to look important or to impose their will on others; they have people cheating each other in business deals; they have people who think it is a good thing to employ the services of prostitutes and others who say even married people should not have sex. On top of all of that, there are people who say there is no resurrection for believers.

All of chapter 15 is dedicated to discussing the resurrection. The people who say there is no resurrection probably believe in an afterlife, just not in the form of a resurrection. Many in the Greco-Roman world saw the soul as superior to the body. Those who believed in post-mortem existence thought that the blessed life would be to exist as a soul without a body so that you are freed from the limitations and distractions a body brings.

But the early church proclaimed that believers would be raised in an embodied form. Much of the reason for this understanding of post-mortem existence was their belief in the resurrection of Christ. If God had raised Christ in a bodily form, then it made sense that believers would be raised to the same sort of existence. The early church did not see the resurrection of Jesus as an isolated event. Holding to an apocalyptic eschatology, they said that Jesus' resurrection was the beginning of the last days. The resurrection of the dead has begun. They expected the end to come soon because the resurrection had begun. Further, the resurrection of Jesus was the creation of a new kind of existence. His resurrection was not the resuscitation of a corpse. It was the creation of a whole new kind of life and a new kind of bodily existence. We will see Paul give expression to this understanding as we examine this text.

Paul begins his discussion of the certainty of the resurrection of believers by reminding the Corinthians of what he says is the central confession of the faith, that Christ died for our sins and was raised in accordance with the Scriptures (15:15). The assertion that Christ was raised was not controversial; everyone in the Corinthian church believes that. After the reminder, he uses their belief in Christ's resurrection to say that it is foolishness to say there is no resurrection of the dead (15:12–19). They already believe in at least one! This paragraph asserts the centrality of the resurrection for the church's faith. If there is no resurrection, then salvation does not come through Christ's death and resurrection, since there cannot be a resurrection. If there is no resurrection, what the church believes is false and the salvation they proclaim is an illusion. That is why they are to be most pitied. No one at Corinth is denying that Jesus was raised. Paul is just drawing out what he wants them to see as a consequence of the claim that there is no resurrection of people to show how foolish and damaging such a claim is. It destroys the faith.

1 Corinthians 15:19-26

Our lection begins with the last verse of that paragraph and moves through the next part of the argument (vv. 20-28). Paul ends his initial connection between the resurrection of believers and that of Christ by saying that if Christ's didn't happen, then their relationship with God is lost. Consequently, church members are the most pitiable people in the world because they accept all the disadvantages of being a believer, and what they believe is a lie.

Verse 20 immediately reasserts that Christ has indeed been raised. Paul then begins to make more connections between Christ's resurrection and that of believers and to talk about the broader meaning of Christ's resurrection. He first says that in the resurrection, Christ is the "first fruits" of those who have died. First fruits is a reference to a sacrifice that is dedicated to God at the very beginning of the harvest. The first sheaf of wheat or first apple is given to God to express thanks for the harvest. The first fruits offering was the initial sample of the coming harvest and it is the assurance that the rest of the crop is coming in. Paul says Christ's resurrection is the sample of the believer's resurrection and the guarantee that it is coming.

After this analogy, Paul assigns the resurrection of Christ an even larger role in God's plan for the cosmos. Paul sets up a typology between Adam and Christ. That is, he develops some correspondences between the significance of Adam and that of Christ. This typology does not seem to have originated with Paul. Others in the early church had said that just as Adam represents the beginning of an era and a mode of existence, so does Christ. But what each era brings is radically different. Drawing on the story of the fall in Genesis 3, Paul says that Adam, a single person, brings death into the world and it affects everyone. That is the pattern. Now Christ, a single person, brings, not death, but resurrection of the dead into the world and it affects everyone. Everyone dies because they live in the realm opened by Adam, those who come into the realm opened by Christ are made alive. This way of thinking about Christ is sometimes called an Adam Christology.

This way of describing the role of Christ gives him cosmic significance. In the Genesis story, the way the world operated changed when Adam sinned. (Those who developed this understanding of Christ did not take into account that in the Genesis narrative Eve is actually the first to sin.) In Genesis 2, no one dies, but after Adam's sin everyone dies. As the cosmos changed so that people die in Adam, in Christ the cosmos changes again. Before Christ no one was raised from the dead, but now that possibility exists for all. So, the death and resurrection of Christ have a cosmic and eschatological role. Christ's resurrection inaugurates the end times.

After introducing this Adam/Christ typology, Paul returns to the analogy of the first fruits. Now he uses it to say that believers do not yet experience the resurrection. The proper order is that the first fruits comes initially and the rest of the harvest comes later. The full possession of resurrection life comes only at the second coming. While believers now participate in the realm that is "in Christ," they do not yet have full possession of the resurrection. This clarification allows Paul to say that the resurrection of the believer's body is in the future even though the believer is already "in Christ."

In vv. 24–28, Paul seems to draw heavily on a preformed tradition, seemingly some known liturgy, as he talks about the victory of Christ over the powers of evil. As he does this, he briefly shifts the focus from the resurrection of believers to what is to happen at the second coming, though the two topics are clearly related. The tradition Paul quotes alludes to Psalm 110:1 to talk about the exalted place of Christ. In this Psalm that is a favorite of the early church, God speaks to the king of Israel and tells him that God is subduing all the king's enemies. The church used this Psalm to speak of the place of Christ. Its reading has God say to Christ that God is subduing the enemies as Christ begins to reign. This is the only place in the New Testament where Christ (rather than God) subdues the powers and puts them under his feet. (This is one of the reasons most see Paul citing a preformed piece here.)

This liturgy has Christ presently reigning, but not yet having subdued all the powers that oppose God's will. When it refers to every "ruler," "authority," and "power," it has in mind beings who oppose God's will. The authority of those powers is manifested in the world through the political, economic, and social structures that do not reflect the justice and goodness that God wants for the world. It is clear that they are still in charge. But this text gives the assurance that they will be defeated. At the end, they will be destroyed in the final exertion of God's resurrecting power. Then all the cosmic powers will be destroyed. In what is perhaps an insertion by Paul, the last of those powers to be defeated will be death (v. 26), the enemy that harms all of God's world.

We should note that when this liturgy asserts that Christ is the one acting to subdue the forces that oppose God's will, it creates a problem for

Paul.¹ When the liturgy quotes Psalm 110:1 in v. 27 it includes, "He put all things under his feet." In a seemingly contorted explanation in vv. 27–28, Paul says that the "all things" subject to Christ does not include God. The usual use of the Psalm does not cause this problem because God is the one subjecting powers and putting them under Christ's feet. Paul cites this tradition to bolster his case, but he also must interpret it so that Christ is always subordinate to God.²

Paul's description of the second coming has Christ turn the kingdom over to God (v. 24). Whoever is subduing the powers, Christ is seen as the one who reigns over all things (other than God) in the cosmos. At the second coming, Christ uses this power to destroy the worst and most powerful enemy of God's will: Death. It is at this point that the power of the resurrection comes to full flower. Then the life-giving power of the resurrection eradicates death. This is what Easter celebrates. It is not the resurrection of Christ as an act done for a single person that is important. The meaning of the resurrection of Christ is that God has power over death and God will exercise that power in the end to give life to all of God's people.

The lectionary ends the reading at v. 26, where Paul declares that Christ will destroy death. This is wonderful note to end on for an Easter message. But this passage does not really end until v. 28. The contorted language of vv. 27–28 may well be enough reason not to make them part of the reading, but the real goal of the second coming comes to clearest expression at the end of v. 28. The purpose of God's eschatological act is to secure the final state of all existence, and that final state is that "God is all in all." That is, all things conform to the character of God. All things then reflect the mercy, goodness, justice, power, and love of God. Part of that proper state of all things is that believers are raised to new life lived in the presence of God.

For a passage that was supposed to support the assertion that the afterlife existence of believers will be embodied, it seems to have gotten a bit off track. What it has said is important for Christian eschatology and theology more broadly. This text affirms God's commitment to us to make all things as they should be. Paul will return more directly to defending

---

1. Making Christ the one who subdues the powers is so strange that the NRSV changes the text by adding the word "God" and so making God the one who subdues the powers. But if the meaning was that God subjected the powers, then the explanation that follows in vv. 27–28 would not be needed or make sense.

2. For a fuller treatment of Paul's use of this liturgy, see Sumney, *Steward of God's Mysteries*, 112–20.

the idea that postmortem existence is as an embodied person in vv. 35–58. Given that our text is a part of the argument for resurrection existence as embodied existence, we might ask why this was so important to the early church and to Paul. We have already noted that this is one way that believers will participate in the life inaugurated in the bodily resurrection of Christ. We saw here how Christ's resurrection existence is the first fruits of the resurrection of all believers.

A second reason bodily resurrection is important is that it invests bodily life with significance. Our lives as embodied persons living in a material world are not insignificant. This view of the resurrection says that embodied existence is the permanent state of human existence. So what our bodies do now matters. Humans are not souls waiting to escape, shedding bodies so that the important part remains. Bodies matter to God and how we live as embodied beings matters to God. Recognizing the embodied nature of all full human existence invests the present with meaning. (Paul will say that those bodies are made of different matter [vv. 42–54], but they will be bodies.) This is why it was important to Paul to argue for the bodily resurrection of believers. The resurrection, then, holds out hope for the future and it endows present life with meaning and significance.

1 Corinthians 15:19-26

IDEAS FOR PREACHING ON 1 CORINTHIANS 15:19-26

Leah D. Schade

An Easter eschatology

Most preachers focus on the Gospel reading for Resurrection Sunday. However, this text from 1 Corinthians 15:19-26 in Year C of the Revised Common Lectionary affords an opportunity to bring an eschatological lens to the celebration of Easter. As Sumney notes, the early church saw Jesus' resurrection not as an isolated event, but as inaugurating the last days. For first-century believers, the resurrection had cosmological and apocalyptic significance, which has direct ramifications for the here and now. "Further, the resurrection of Jesus was the creation of a new kind of existence. His resurrection was not the resuscitation of a corpse. It was the creation of a whole new kind of life and a new kind of bodily existence," says Sumney.

The preacher will want to ask: what does this new kind of life look like? In what ways can we experience this new kind of bodily existence even as we're living in the midst of Good Fridays and Saturday Vigils? How can the "already" of Jesus' resurrection sustain us during the "not yet" as we await the Parousia? The sermon can answer these questions by including stories and images that illustrate the church and the Christian community living out a resurrection faith in powerful and life-changing ways. For example, I once served a church where a father and son were in a serious car accident that nearly ended their lives and left them with serious injuries. But the church instantly came together to provide funds for the wife and the rest of the family, brought them meals, prayed, and visited with them. After many long weeks, the father and son returned to church. The father was barely able to walk, but he and the congregation praised God for the "already" of new life, even if the "not yet" of healing was not entirely fulfilled.

Beware of "trolls"

Sumney explains that Paul's letter to the Corinthians aims to shut down the claim by some in the early church that there is no physical resurrection. Not only is such a claim silly, it is also harmful. Today there is no shortage of people who not only argue against a bodily resurrection, but also claim that the resurrection of Christ never happened in the first place. In fact, there are even some who argue that Jesus of Nazareth never existed at all. We might call them "spiritual trolls." In online and social media platforms, trolls are people who stir up controversy, aggravate others, and intentionally create negative feelings. I know of one person who trolls through the blogsite I write for finding every opportunity to post memes about how Jesus is not a real historical figure and that the resurrection is fiction. He's made it his mission to sow doubts about Christianity everywhere he can. He's one of many such trolls.

Paul encountered trolls in his own time. But they weren't just coming from outside of the church. They were congregation members who were sowing doubts about the claim that Christians will share in Christ's resurrection. Paul's letter to the church in Corinth devotes a whole chapter to taking down their arguments. Why does he spend so much time on this? Because he knows that what they are doing undermines the church. Worse, trolling is dangerous because it tries to destroy people's faith.

This is not to say that Christians have to shut down their critical thinking skills and accept everything with unquestioning faith. Preachers wanting to engage in apologetics about the mystery of the resurrection will need to be clear that it's a good thing to wrestle with what the resurrection means for our lives. But those who troll are not interested in dialogue. Their aim is to be deliberatively provocative and offensive in order to upset people. They take wicked delight in stirring up anger and confusion. We might say that this is a form of "spiritual gaslighting."[3] The sermon, then, can offer a ballast for those whose faith has been shaken by such mean-spiritedness. Differentiating between honest questions and doubts versus gaslighting and trolling can be enlightening and empowering.

---

3. Gaslighting is the attempt of one person to overwrite another person's reality. It is a tactic used for gaining power and control. The term gets its name from a 1938 play and 1944 film *Gaslight*, starring Ingrid Bergman, in which her husband secretly dimmed the gaslight, but when she commented on it, he insisted she must be crazy. And he convinced others she was insane as well. Thus, gaslighting is a form of manipulation through persistent denial, misdirection, contradiction, and lying in an attempt to destabilize and delegitimize a person or group of people.

1 Corinthians 15:19–26

Putting rulers, authorities, and powers in their proper place

In verse 24, Paul expands the ramifications of the resurrection beyond individual bodies to include "rulers, authorities and powers"—clearly moving into a more political realm. Walter Wink, in his book *Engaging the Powers: Discernment and Resistance in a World of Domination*, notes:

> The Powers are not simply evil. They are a bulwark against anarchy, and a patron, repository, and inspirer of art. They inculcate values that encourage interdependency, mutual care, and social cohesiveness. They encourage submission of personal desires to the general good of everyone. Their evil is not intrinsic, but rather the result of idolatry.[4]

He describes a drama surrounding the Powers in the New Testament in this way: "the Powers are good, the Powers are Fallen, the Powers will be redeemed."[5] Sumney notes that "the authority of those powers is manifested in the world through the political, economic, and social structures that do not reflect the justice and goodness that God wants for the world. It is clear that they are still in charge." Preachers can help their listeners identify the rulers, authorities, and powers that oppose God's will in our own time.

For example, what are the political structures that enable the powerful to control people through manipulation, fear, and violence? What are the economic structures that allow for the gross accumulation of wealth by a handful of individuals while 90 percent of the world struggles to make ends meet? Why is it acceptable that 10 percent of the world lives in such extreme poverty they must try to live on less than $2 a day?[6] In what ways are sexism, racism, homophobia, and ableism, for example, built into the social structures that form our everyday lives? The sermon can give evidence that God is working through entities such as the church, community organizers, and people of faith aligned with the values of Christ's realm in order to bring accountability to the Powers. In this way, we can loosen the Powers' hold on people and the systems that structure our lives until Christ returns to restore justice fully and completely.

---

4. Wink, *Engaging the Powers*, 65.
5. Wink, *Engaging the Powers*, 65.
6. The World Bank, "Poverty Overview."

Apocalypse When?

"THE FLESHY FAITH OF RESURRECTION: AN EASTER SERMON"

A Sermon on Luke 24:1–12; 1 Cor 15:19–26

Leah D. Schade

Sometimes Jesus shows up in the darnedest places. Who would have thought that the Son of God would show up in the womb of an unmarried teenage girl living on the outskirts of the Roman Empire in a little backwater town called Nazareth? And when the baby was born in a dusty barn on the outskirts of Bethlehem, the fact was so startling a whole host of angels had to be sent to a group of shepherds with the news.

Yes, it's shocking. Yes, it's unconventional. Yes, it's completely unexpected. But God's Son is coming here, to you, at this very moment. Sometimes Jesus shows up in the darnedest places.

On this Easter morning, we hear the story of Jesus showing up, once again, in the darndest place. Who would have expected Jesus to show up on that Sunday morning outside of his own tomb on the outskirts of Jerusalem after having been crucified in the city dump three days before? The fact was so startling that an angel had to be sent to the women who had come to anoint his body and mourn his death. And the message given to those women? "Why do you look for the living among the dead? He is not here, but has risen. Remember how he told you, while he was still in Galilee, that the Son of Man must be handed over to sinners, and be crucified, and on the third day rise again." Yes, it's shocking. Yes, it's unconventional. Yes, it's completely unexpected. But God's resurrected Son is coming here, to you, at this very moment. Sometimes Jesus shows up in the darnedest places.

And when Jesus shows up, it means something incredible for our world, for our future, and for our very bodies. Because of Christ's incarnation, crucifixion, and resurrection, we know that our bodies mean something to God. Mary's body carrying Jesus' body meant something to God. All the people whom Jesus healed and fed—their bodies meant something to him. Your body, our bodies here in this place—they mean something to God.

There are, of course, some who would dispute this idea. Even the first Christians were not certain what the resurrection meant for them. In fact, when Paul wrote this letter to the church in Corinth, he was writing to people who did not believe that their own bodies would be resurrected in the final days of Christ's return. Oh, sure, they believed that Jesus was raised from the dead. But they did not believe there would be a physical resurrection for them.

Why would they want their bodies resurrected, anyway? Bodies feel pain. They get sick and suffer injuries. They get flabby and wrinkly. Sometimes they stink! The Greeks believed that the body was inferior to the soul, so the afterlife would consist of their spirits freed from these fleshy, imperfect, smelly containers.

But Paul explains to them that they're thinking about this in the wrong way: "For since death came through a human being, the resurrection of the dead has also come through a human being; for as all die in Adam, so all will be made alive in Christ" (1 Cor 15:21–22). Paul is saying that our bodies matter so much that they will be resurrected, along with Christ. Why is this important? Because if this flesh, this matter, the atoms and molecules that make up who we are—if this is all just a shell that we shed when we die, if Earth is just a container that will be thrown away when Christ returns—then there is truly no reason to care about them now.

But Paul is very clear that the resurrection of our bodies means that we matter to God. *Matter* matters to God. And what we do with this matter—our bodies, other people's bodies, the body of our Earth—matters to God as well. When we grasp both the cosmic and local significance of this, it makes a difference in how we act and what we do with these fragile, precious bodies.

Take for instance, Rev. Fred Small, who was one of the first faith leaders to engage in civil disobedience to draw attention to climate change. In 2015, he left parish ministry to devote his energies to climate advocacy, serving as Minister for Climate Justice at Arlington Street Church, Boston. He does this because of his faith, because he knows that God cares about our bodies, cares for Earth's body.

In a book I co-edited called *Rooted and Rising: Voices of Courage in a Time of Climate Crisis*, Rev. Small tells the story of when he was arrested in 2016 in an act of civil disobedience protesting the fracked gas pipeline that was being constructed in West Roxbury, a neighborhood of Boston. "Residents were worried about potential leaks and explosions, as well as about the pipeline's contribution to global warming," he said. "Before the action, seventy of us gathered for interfaith worship at Theodore Parker Church in West Roxbury. We shared our grief for the Earth and all those suffering upon it. We prayed. We sang."[7]

Like women going to the tomb on that Easter morning to care for the body of their crucified friend and teacher, a small group went to the trench where Earth's body was being gashed for this pipeline. "In solidarity with the Standing Rock Sioux in their struggle against the Dakota Access Pipeline, ten of us blocked construction in West Roxbury by either sitting on the edge of the trench or climbing down into it."[8]

But then something unexpected happened. "As the police arrested us, one of them whispered, 'Thank you for your service.'" Right there in the pipeline trench, Jesus was there with the protestors, and with the policeman. "Thank you for your service." Sometimes Jesus shows up in the darnedest places.

Where have you seen Jesus show up in unexpected places and unconventional ways?

I remember an interview I heard with a woman who was caught in the 2016 bombing of the airport in Brussels, Belgium. She admitted that when the bombs first went off, she was terrified and spent the first moments of the aftermath hiding under a table. "Frankly, I was a coward," she said. But then she saw two little girls injured and in need of care and attention. So she went to them, sang songs, and said the Lord's Prayer with them, until medical help could arrive. Right there, in the midst of hell on earth, Jesus showed up in the midst of the smoke and rubble, singing through this woman's tremulous voice. Their bodies mattered to God. This woman's faith compelled her and gave her the courage in that moment to be a holy presence for those girls. Jesus shows up in the darndest places.

Where might Jesus show up for you? Where will you encounter the risen Christ who fills you with courage? It won't always be big, heroic acts. It won't necessarily be in a bombed-out airport or a muddy pipeline trench. It may be in the simple, everyday acts like Mary diapering her baby—just as many of you have diapered and cared for children. Or in feeding a hungry crowd on a hillside, their bellies growling—just as many of you have prepared meals for others. Or Jesus may show up as he did day in and day out with the disciples, talking with them, being present with them, teaching them how to pray.

---

7. Small, "Praise Be the Flood," 33.
8. Small, "Praise Be the Flood," 33.

1 Corinthians 15:19-26

This is what Vivian discovered in her work as a hospice volunteer. Vivian was one of my parishioners, and day in and day out she visited patients who were approaching the end of their lives. She told me about one particular woman she was visiting who was in an advanced stage of dementia. The woman was in a nursing home, seated in one of those large rolling chairs outside the nurses' station. The woman had not been able to talk sensibly or in complete sentences for over a year.

On this particular day, Vivian sat down with her and patiently listened to the woman rambling on, as she usually did, not making much sense. But then Vivian thought she heard the woman say the word *church*. So she asked, "Did you like to go to church?" The woman stopped talking and got very calm.

"I'll bet that means that you said a lot of prayers," Vivian said. The woman perked up and said, "Prayer! Prayer!" Vivian held her hand and asked, "Would you like to pray?" The woman nodded, so Vivian began, "Our Father, who art in heaven." And this woman *who had not said a complete sentence in over a year* said the entire Lord's Prayer, the prayer that Jesus taught us, as Vivian prayed along with her.

Two days later, the woman died. But in that moment, Jesus showed up for her—and for Vivian. Their bodies, their voices, their prayers mattered to God.

Who would have thought that Jesus would show up on that day in a nursing home for a woman about to face her own death? But Vivian's presence was like the message of the angel for that woman. God's Son is coming here, to you, at this very moment. Sometimes Jesus shows up in the darnedest places.

My friends, ours is not a disembodied faith floating around in the ether. It is a fleshy faith. It is a holding hands in the nursing home faith. It is a sitting in the trenches faith. It is a faith of bodies who show up in the darndest places proclaiming Christ crucified and resurrected, proclaiming Earth's body crucified and resurrected, proclaiming with Paul that "the last enemy to be destroyed is death" (v. 26).

When you receive this bread and wine today, think of the places where you can carry this message out into the world, telling people not to be afraid, assuring them with a gentle touch and a hopeful word from God. The brows creased with worry or anger that need the news of Christ's presence. The hands cracked and blistered from work that pays too little and demands too much. The halls of governments, the corporate offices that need to know the news that the resurrected Christ demands justice for God's people.

And remember that Christ's presence is for your creased brow, your blistered hands, your tired feet as well. Jesus shows up for you in the same way. Remember this when you hold the bread and cup in your hand. What Jesus offers to the world is given to you as well.

Jesus meets us unexpectedly, completely without warning. In the pastures of shepherds and feeding stalls of dusty barns, in hospital rooms and bombed-out airports and pipeline trenches. Jesus shows up in the darnedest places. Yes, it's shocking. Yes, it's unconventional. Yes, it's completely unexpected. But God's Son, the risen Christ, is coming here, to you, at this very moment. Thanks be to God.

Chapter 8

1 Thessalonians 4:13–18

(Year A—Season after Pentecost—Proper 27 [32])

> ¹³But we do not want you to be uninformed, brothers and sisters, about those who have died, so that you may not grieve as others do who have no hope. ¹⁴For since we believe that Jesus died and rose again, even so, through Jesus, God will bring with him those who have died. ¹⁵For this we declare to you by the word of the Lord, that we who are alive, who are left until the coming of the Lord, will by no means precede those who have died. ¹⁶For the Lord himself, with a cry of command, with the archangel's call and with the sound of God's trumpet, will descend from heaven, and the dead in Christ will rise first. ¹⁷Then we who are alive, who are left, will be caught up in the clouds together with them to meet the Lord in the air; and so we will be with the Lord forever. ¹⁸Therefore encourage one another with these words.

AN EXEGESIS OF 1 THESSALONIANS 4:13–18

Jerry L. Sumney

First Thessalonians is probably the earliest writing in the New Testament, most likely written around the year 51. It addresses a congregation that was very young and had experienced significant persecution. One of the main reasons Paul writes this letter is to provide them with an interpretation of that experience which affirms their faith in Christ. The specific occasion of Paul's writing is the return of Timothy from visiting the Thessalonians. Paul had been worried about them and so sent Timothy to see how they were holding up in his absence. Timothy reports that they are maintaining their faith, despite the difficult circumstances they are encountering. Writing from Corinth, Paul praises them for their faithfulness, responds to some questions they have sent to him, and comments on some areas in which they need to grow (3:10). Their questions involve eschatology. Specifically, they want to know about the fate of believers who die before the Parousia[1] and they want some information about when that second coming will happen.

Like all first-generation church members, the Thessalonians believed that the second coming of Christ was very near. The earliest church understood the resurrection of Christ to be the beginning of the resurrection of all the dead at the judgment. Since the Last Days had been inaugurated with the resurrection of Christ, surely God would complete the act begun with that resurrection. Surely, God was ready to set the world aright. When they first experienced opposition and persecution, that made them even more sure that God would act to end the suffering of the faithful. By the time Paul writes 1 Thessalonians, the church has been looking for the end for nearly two decades. By then, the wider church had developed some ways of understanding the delay, but the Thessalonians seemingly did not know about them. They seem to have thought that Christ would return to defeat evil before anyone in their church died. Thus, when some in their church died, they were concerned that those fellow church members would miss the Parousia. Apparently, Paul had not given them instruction about this matter before he left town. The wider church had seen many members die by this time, including some who were martyred. So, the church had already been forced the think about this matter. This means Paul can rely on what others have already said about the delay of the second coming and about the fate of those who die before the end.

Since Paul says he does not want the Thessalonians to have the same grief as those "who have no hope" (v. 13), they may have thought that those who die before the second coming had no afterlife. Many people in the first century did not think that humans had any post-mortem existence. If the

---

1. *Parousia* is the word sometimes used in the New Testament to refer to the second coming of Christ.

1 Thessalonians 4:13-18

Thessalonians don't worry that their fellow-believers are just dead, they are at least worried that those who died would miss the blessings associated with the event of the second coming. This problem is acute because this church is being persecuted. It is even possible that some had died because of the persecution. In circumstances like this, worries about whether a person is excluded from the blessings of being in God's presence are especially important. After all, if there is no assurance of participating in that life with God, why would you continue to endure persecution now? Paul's answer to the question about the fate of those who have died must assure the Thessalonians that God's treatment of them more than makes up for their experience of persecution.

As he does elsewhere (e.g., 1 Corinthians 15), Paul begins his response to questions about the resurrection of believers by tying it to the resurrection of Christ. Paul is convinced that Christ's resurrection is the model for and the assurance of the resurrection of believers. Since God raised Christ, God will raise those who trust in Christ for their relationship with God. The point he stresses in 4:14 is that the belief that God raised Christ entails the belief that God will raise believers with him. The life of believers is so closely identified with Christ that they will share in his resurrection life.

In 4:15 Paul identifies what follows in vv. 15-17 as a "word of the Lord," that is, as material which the tradition traced back to sayings of Jesus.[2] Many interpreters think Paul is drawing on the same traditions which informed the "Synoptic Apocalypse," especially those used to write Matthew 24, because of the similarities of features and vocabulary. It is important to remember that Paul's point is not to set out the exact chronology of all things associated with the Parousia. Rather his main point is to respond to questions about the fate of those believers who die before it. This is clear from the first words which follow his identification of what he is about to say as a word of the Lord: at the Parousia, the living will not precede those who have died. This is the one point of chronology Paul wants to establish. If he can convince them of this, he can allay much of their concern about both the fate of those who die and their worry about the delay in Christ's return.

The imagery Paul uses in v. 16 is commonly found in apocalyptic writings. In this verse he lists three events that are parallel within the structure

---

2. Though some think this may be a word of the risen Christ received by early church prophets, it seems much more likely (especially given its parallels with Matthew 24) that Paul knows this as a tradition he has received as a saying of the earthly Jesus. See the discussion in Sumney, *Steward of God's Mysteries*, 104-12.

of this sentence. With this structure Paul presents the Lord coming down from the clouds, the archangel's voice, and the trumpet of God (these are also found in Matthew 24:30–31) all as part of the Parousia and as happening simultaneously. The angel's call and the trumpet can signal that a message is coming from God or they can announce the presence of God. They seem to do the latter here. The only chronological note in this opening description is in the last clause of the verse: believers who have died will be the first to participate in the Parousia. According to v. 17, it is only after the dead have been raised and are already with Christ that those who are still alive at the time of the second coming will join Christ in the clouds. Paul's first response to their worry, then, is to say that those who have died not only don't miss what those who live until the end get, they also begin to participate in that event before those who are still alive.

When Paul speaks of those who are still alive at the Parousia in v. 17, he uses the pronoun "we." While it is possible that "we" is something like an editorial we, Paul may well have expected to live to see the second coming when he wrote this letter. By the time he writes 2 Corinthians (5:15) and Philippians (1:19–26) at least five years later, he thinks he may die before the return of Christ. But at this early time, he may think he will live to see it.

This is one of the passages from which some readers develop the idea of the Rapture. The verb translated "caught up" (NRSV) is the Greek word *harpazō* which is translated into Latin as *rapere*, the word from which we get "rapture." We should note that this word is a verb, not a noun. Thus, it is used to describe what is happening; the New Testament never calls any event "the Rapture." What Paul describes here has nothing to do with a "Rapture" in which the good people are whisked away and the bad people are left to suffer. Paul is here describing the end of the world as we know it; this is Judgment Day. It is important to note that this transporting of the believers into the clouds to meet Christ happens immediately *after* the resurrection of the dead and is part of the one event that is the second coming, the consummation of all things. The taking up of the faithful is not a prelude to the Parousia but a part of it.

This is one of those places where we need to reclaim a text from those who use it to frighten and intimidate. Those who talk about the "Rapture" use it to scare people into the faith and then to congratulate themselves on being among those who will certainly not suffer in its aftermath. This text has absolutely nothing to say about a scenario that has God snatch the good people out of the world so that the bad people can suffer for 1,000 years.

Careful attention to this text can inoculate us from the attempts to make this a text that frightens us. Reading so that we see that this passage describes the final resurrection means that it cannot be a part of a "Rapture" scheme. The being "taken up" here is the promise that the life of faith will certainly include life with the risen Christ in an existence that transcends the troubles of the world.

There is a tension in this passage between Christ coming down from heaven and believers being taken up to Christ. Given the movement in both directions (up and down), it is not clear whether the eventual abode of believers with Christ is on earth or in a heavenly realm. While we may want clarity about this, it does not matter to the point Paul is making. Wherever that existence with God is, the Thessalonians can be certain that those who have died and those who have been persecuted participate in it fully.

In v. 17 Paul closes this description of the end by asserting that the final result of all this action is that those who have died and those who are alive at the Parousia will, following that moment, be with the Lord always. This foundational belief and trust in the faithfulness of God is what all else in this passage is built on.

The section ends on a note of exhortation. The portrait of the second coming Paul has sketched is to be used to comfort and encourage those in the church community. When we remember that these people are persecuted for their confession of Christ, these words are important as comfort. They assure the suffering that God has not deserted them and that even death cannot separate them from God and cannot keep God from fulfilling God's loving purposes with them. God will gather them to Godself forever. As they remind one another of the certainty of life with God, that remembering is intended to motivate them to be able to live for God. It is intended to help them endure persecution.

This exhortation is also important as we think about this passage. It is sometimes said that talking about eschatology and particularly life beyond our present existence is a kind of escapism. There is the worry that looking to that future will keep believers from being concerned about life in this world. If that is what happens, the people have lost sight of what talk about eschatology is supposed to do. Throughout the New Testament, authors talk about the future life with God as a way to motivate the readers to live for God now. Discussion of life beyond this world is supposed to help us put the present into perspective. This is the time of living for God and working for what God wants in the world. Often, for the earliest church nearly always, working to make the world more of what God wants it to be brings disadvantage when measured according to the cultural, economic, and political standards that structure our world. Talk of life with God beyond this realm should remind Christians that we can accept, even take on voluntarily, those disadvantages because we know that the final nature of our existence will more than make up for any disadvantages we accept in this life.

1 Thessalonians 4:13-18

IDEAS FOR PREACHING ON 1 THESSALONIANS 4:13-18

Leah D. Schade

Liturgical context for 1 Thessalonians

In the Revised Common Lectionary, this text from First Thessalonians, along with Chapter 5 that follows, are read in Year A during the last two Sundays of Pentecost before Christ the King Sunday. In terms of the calendar, this places them sometime in the month of November, just prior to the Thanksgiving holiday. For many, the holidays can be a time of sadness in remembering those who no longer share our tables due to divorce, illness, moving away, or death. The preacher may find this text to be an ideal opportunity to speak about grief and loss, as well as Paul's promise of comfort for those who mourn.

The sermon can explore what it might look like for the congregation to "encourage one another with these words" (v. 18). How might individuals, as well as the church as a whole, embody the presence of the risen Christ? What ministries help us to communicate that, as Sumney says, "God has not deserted them and that even death cannot separate them from God and cannot keep God from fulfilling God's loving purposes with them"? This may be an ideal Sunday to commission or reaffirm the ministries of those who visit the sick, Stephen Ministers, those who bring communion to the homebound, a congregation's prison ministry, or those who knit prayer shawls for people in need.

Preaching in the face of commercialized eschatology

Given the increasing preponderance of eschatological fiction on bookshelves, in movie theatres, and on people's personal screens, preaching on 1 Thessalonians 4 poses interesting challenges. Preachers will need to be aware that within their congregations there are some who either firmly believe in the false teachings of end-time proponents, or have consumed one of the many books, movies, or videos manufactured by the apocalypse industry. Others will know of friends or family members who have done so.

The temptation may be to poke holes in such beliefs or launch into a polemical corrective of such twisted theology in the sermon. A more pastoral approach, however, is to acknowledge the *feelings* that underlie and accompany people's reactions to world events that can lead some to cling to these interpretations of biblical prophecy. In preparing the sermon, it will be important to recognize the *fear* that feeds much of the hysteria and obsession around commercialized eschatology. One way to do this is to point to the parallels between the world of the text and our own world today.

As Sumney points out, this first letter to the Thessalonians was addressed to a congregation that had undergone a great deal of persecution: "One of the main reasons Paul writes this letter is to provide them with an interpretation of that experience which affirms their faith in Christ." Similarly, the preacher will want to find a way to affirm their listeners' faith in God, even if some are misguided in their pursuit of end-time theories.

When the world seems out of control, and when headlines seem to mirror biblical apocalyptic scenarios, it is natural to want to find a hidden meaning buried within the chaos and to unearth clues as to what God has in mind for this mess. We see that the people of Thessalonica had similar concerns. Their questions are our questions: What happens to believers who die before the return of Christ? When is Jesus coming back to end this horrific madness and save us from suffering?

And like the Thessalonians, many today believe that the second coming of Christ is coming very, very soon. It's natural to want to see a happy ending to this story in our lifetimes. We feed on superhero movies where the good guys defeat the bad guys and wrap things up in about 180 minutes. Who can blame us for wanting to see an end to corruption, poverty, racism, violence, and the threat of war within the next few years? In other words, the preacher can name the *longing* for God's justice, even when that longing is manipulated and commodified for enormous profit.

Blessed assurance

New Testament theologian Barbara Rossing emphasizes that "biblical prophets are not predictors of end-times events, they are inspired voices calling people to repentance and justice. They tell the wonderful and crucial story of God's faithfulness. They give us hope."[3] This hope is key to proclamation of this text.

---

3. Rossing, *The Rapture Exposed*, xvii.

1 Thessalonians 4:13–18

Without belittling or berating misplaced enthusiasm for biblical prophecy, the preacher can help design a worship service that reinforces Paul's message in this text. Through hymns, prayers, anointing with oil, and Holy Communion, our rituals can buttress the proclamation that everyone—living, dead, and still to be born—will be together with each other and with Christ. As Rossing reminds us, "Paul is saying the very opposite of what Rapture proponents claim when they use him to support their terrifying left-behind notion that some people will be taken while others are left. Paul's pastoral concern here is to comfort people by showing that we will all be together in Christ when he comes again. We will not be separated from Christ or from one another."[4] May our preaching amplify this message.

---

4. Rossing, *The Rapture Exposed*, 175.

Apocalypse When?

"THE PASTORAL VISIT"

A Sermon on 1 Thessalonians 4:13–18

Leah D. Schade

(This sermon tells the story of "Pastor Jarvis" and "Miss Diane," a pastoral colleague of mine and her parishioner who engage in a conversation about Left Behind *theology. The names and details of the story are changed to protect anonymity, but the essence of the story is retained.)*

Miss Diane's house smelled of pine cleaner and freshly dried laundry, with just a hint of moth balls. Pastor Jarvis noticed this the first time she visited her parishioner to bring her communion and share with her the Sunday bulletin from church. Miss Diane lived in the in-law quarters of her son's house ever since her bout with cancer had left her physically depleted. The tiny quarters were kept neat and clean by Mindy, her caregiver. Mindy made her lunch and always checked that Miss Diane's television was tuned to either her favorite soap opera or the Christian station before she left for the day.

As she did each visit, Pastor Jarvis came in and set down her communion carrier on the little TV tray next to Miss Diane's favorite overstuffed chair with the bright, cheery flowers. The green prayer shawl knitted by someone from the church was neatly folded over the armrest. On the side table was Miss Diane's Scofield Bible alongside her favorite book, *Left Behind: A Novel of the Earth's Last Days,* by Tim LaHaye and Jerry B. Jenkins.

"I mean, just imagine, Pastor," Miss Diane said with wonderment in her voice. "Imagine being at the grocery store, or the hairdressers, or sitting in the movie theater when all of a sudden, the person next to you just disappears. And another person across the room, and another and another. All those people are just gone without a trace, caught up in the clouds to meet Jesus. Won't that be wonderful?"

Pastor Jarvis wasn't quite sure how to respond. She had read *Left Behind* at Miss Diane's insistence, wanting to understand her parishioner's fervor for the book. At the story's beginning, Captain Rayford Steele is piloting his airplane in mid-flight when people suddenly disappear into thin air. All that's left are the clothes they were wearing. Of course, there is mass

1 Thessalonians 4:13–18

hysteria as those "left behind" discover that they have just experienced something called the Rapture.

"I don't know, Miss Diane," the pastor said carefully. "I think that would be pretty scary."

"Oh, you and I won't need to worry about that," said the woman, waving away the thought. "We're believers. We're going to be with Jesus. I just feel so sorry for all those Muslims who don't know Jesus. And all the Jews, although they'll get a second chance to come to Jesus during the Tribulation."

According to the book, the Tribulation is part of "the judgment of God on an ungodly world." In one chapter, a minister explains in the videotape he kindly left behind for the poor folks remaining after the Rapture that this is "God's final effort to get the attention of every person who has ignored or rejected him. He is allowing now a vast period of trial and tribulation to come to you who remain."[5] All of this is God's last-ditch attempt to get people to convert to Christianity or be doomed to hell forever.

"See here, Pastor," Miss Diane said, opening her Bible to chapter 4 of Paul's First Letter to the Thessalonians. She read verses 16 and 17: "For the Lord himself, with a cry of command, with the archangel's call and with the sound of God's trumpet, will descend from heaven, and the dead in Christ will rise first. Then we who are alive, who are left, will be caught up in the clouds together with them to meet the Lord in the air."

"Hm. What does that verse mean to you?" the pastor asked.

"Why, it's all right here, don't you see? All of this is part of God's great plan in the Bible."

"All of *what* is part of God's plan?" asked Pastor Jarvis.

"Everything—the hijackings on September 11, the fighting in the Middle East, the earthquakes, the hurricanes—it's all happening just as the prophecies predicted."

Now, if I had been the pastor visiting Miss Diane, I would have had a difficult time holding back my urge to debunk everything that this woman was saying. *Left Behind* is part of a genre called "apocalyptic fiction" that imagines stories of the end times loosely based on a particular interpretation of certain biblical passages. The first *Left Behind* book was written in 1995 and was part of a series of sixteen books that also led to movies and even a video game. The enterprise has generated millions of dollars and

---

5. LaHaye and Jenkins, *Left Behind*, 212.

fomented an ongoing obsession with envisioning the end of the world. And it all revolves around this highly anticipated event called the Rapture.

These ideas were first proposed by a man named John Nelson Darby in 1833. He suggested that the second coming of Christ will come in stages called "dispensations." In the first stage, Christ will come to judge the world. All those who are born-again Christians will be lifted into the air and united with him in a moment of pure *rapture*, an intense experience of joy and bliss. But those who are "left behind" will face a period of intense tribulation, chaos, massive upheaval, and the despotic reign of a figure called the Anti-Christ.

Now, some may chuckle uncomfortably at such an idea. But others believe in their heart of hearts that this is exactly how the world will end. You may know people for whom this story of the Rapture is foundational for their faith. Maybe you yourself have wondered if perhaps there's something to all this talk about the end times, given the present state of our world.

But if I had been visiting Miss Diane, I would not have been as patient as my colleague Pastor Jarvis. I would have wanted to tell the woman that New Testament scholars have unanimously concluded these interpretations of the Bible are based on pure fiction. "These end-times writings draw on a method for looking at prophecy that was invented less than two hundred years ago," writes Barbara Rossing in her book *The Rapture Exposed: The Message of Hope in the Book of Revelation*.[6] This method involves trying to decode a supposedly hidden message in the Bible telling us when the world will end and then to discover the signs that indicate such an end is coming.

I remember as a kid when some of my family members would tell me about the hidden codes in Scripture. They told me that there is a whole system for figuring out the meaning of certain numbers, words, and symbols in the Bible. They showed me elaborate equations written in their Bibles. Certain pages were highlighted with cryptic numbering and clues. They gave me fantastical books to read where invisible angels and demons were fighting a cosmic battle alongside human beings but on a different plane of existence. And these two realms were colliding as the world unraveled.

When I became a pastor, I learned that it wasn't just my family members who espoused these end-time theories. A few parishioners would slip me books—best-selling titles—purporting to reveal "the truth" about the Bible. They would share videos with me from "biblical experts" explaining

---

6. Rossing, *The Rapture Exposed*, xvii.

1 Thessalonians 4:13–18

the real meaning of political events and how they were predicted by biblical prophecy.

I'll admit, there is something intriguing about trying to unearth the clues of biblical fortune-telling. It's like reading a mystery novel where you're attempting to figure out what's going on, what's going to happen, and how it's all going to turn out. Or it's like a puzzle, and the key to unlocking the solution is confessing Jesus Christ as your personal Lord and Savior. Only those who have accepted a certain form of Christianity can obtain the secret knowledge that will allow them to figure out the chronology of the end times. Everyone else is in danger of being overcome by the wrath of God and losing their very souls.

Knowing all this, if I had been visiting Miss Diane, I would have wanted to correct her. I would have wanted to tell her that God didn't intend for the Bible to be a collection of puzzle pieces or clues in a mystery. I would have told her that biblical prophets did not intend to predict end-time events. They wanted to call people to repentance and justice for this world, right here and now.

But, fortunately, I was not the one visiting Miss Diane. Pastor Jarvis was. And when her parishioner went on about all the upheaval going on in the world and its connection to prophecies in the Bible, Pastor Jarvis was much more pastoral than I would have been. She said, "I agree, it is really awful what's going on these days. Sometimes I lie awake at night worrying about all the violence and what kind of world my kids are going to grow up in. What's worrying you these days, Miss Diane?"

After a moment's hesitation, she replied, "The cancer. I mean, I know I'm going to be with Jesus. But I worry all the time that the cancer is going to come back. Now, I know God will give me strength. But I just don't know if I can go through that again."

Just like that, my pastoral colleague had gotten to the heart of the matter with her parishioner. She listened without being judgmental. And she validated how the woman was feeling. This opened the door for Miss Diane to share what was bothering her. And in that moment, there was a connection between them. They talked at length about the fear she felt every time she went to the doctor for a check-up and how she felt like a burden to her son. But also, she talked about how grateful she was for Mindy who did so much for her and would sit with her sometimes to watch her shows or read to her from the Bible or the *Left Behind* book.

"That girl is a Godsend, I'll tell you what," said Miss Diane. "She has opened the Scripture to me and helped me understand God's plan in all of this. Why, she could have been a pastor, just like you!"

At this point in the conversation, I would have felt pretty ticked off at Mindy. *She's* the one who got Miss Diane into all this biblical prophecy stuff. She's taking advantage of a poor, vulnerable woman, I would have been thinking to myself.

But Pastor Jarvis took it in stride. "Tell me why else you feel Mindy is a Godsend," she said. Miss Diane told her how Mindy made sure her bed was made just the way she liked it with the blanket tucked neatly under the pillows. And how she was patient, a good listener, and knew her Bible.

"It sounds like Mindy brings you a lot of comfort," said the pastor.

"Oh, she does! Just like you do!" she added.

Then Pastor Jarvis did something I would not have thought to do. She made a connection back to the biblical text. She said, "Did you know that the people Paul was writing to in Thessalonians were also dealing with some really difficult times? They were being killed for their faith. They lived with fear daily, just like you do."

"Now that's something I didn't know," Miss Diane said.

"They didn't understand why Jesus hadn't come back yet. So Paul's letter was meant to comfort them, to give them hope," said Pastor Jarvis.

"Well," said Ms. Diane, "I guess that's what I'm looking for, too. Hope."

"I'm the same way," said the pastor. "That's why communion is so important to me. It reminds me that since God resurrected Jesus from death, God will raise us as well."

"Oh, yes," said Miss Diane. "Are you going to get out that little cup and plate now?" she asked with a smile.

The pastor set out the bread and the cup. "And what Paul is saying," she said as the sweet liquid poured into the cup, "is that it all happens together. Christ's return, those who died in faith rising again, and those of us still alive—all of us meet Jesus at the same time. That's what I remember when I take the bread and cup. I remember that we're all together, all people of all time."

"Well, I don't know about that," the woman said doubtfully. "The Bible says there will be a time of suffering for those left behind—a thousand years! I read it in the book of Revelation!"

Pastor Jarvis smiled and held out her hands in prayer. "In the night in which he was betrayed, our Lord Jesus took bread, broke it and gave to all to eat saying: 'This is my body given for you. Do this in remembrance of me...'"

After they had eaten the bread, sipped from the cup, and said the final prayer, my colleague went to the sink to wash the tiny chalice and paten. She came back to find Miss Diane holding a framed picture of her son and daughter-in-law holding a chubby-cheeked baby boy.

"My grandson would have been ten years old this year," the woman said, her finger lightly touching the glass.

"The pain never goes away, does it?" Pastor Jarvis asked.

"No," whispered Miss Diane. "But I know he's already with God. And I'll see him soon enough. That's what the Bible says."

"That *is* what the Bible says," my colleague agreed. "Paul says, 'we will be with the Lord forever. Therefore encourage one another with these words.'"

Pastor Jarvis encouraged Miss Diane with those words. I hope you will be encouraged as well. Amen.

Chapter 9

1 Thessalonians 5:1–11
(Year A—Season after Pentecost—Proper 28 [33])

¹*Now concerning the times and the seasons, brothers and sisters, you do not need to have anything written to you.* ²*For you yourselves know very well that the day of the Lord will come like a thief in the night.* ³*When they say, "There is peace and security," then sudden destruction will come upon them, as labor pains come upon a pregnant woman, and there will be no escape!* ⁴*But you, beloved, are not in darkness, for that day to surprise you like a thief;* ⁵*for you are all children of light and children of the day; we are not of the night or of darkness.*

⁶*So then let us not fall asleep as others do, but let us keep awake and be sober;* ⁷*for those who sleep sleep at night, and those who are drunk get drunk at night.* ⁸*But since we belong to the day, let us be sober, and put on the breastplate of faith and love, and for a helmet the hope of salvation.* ⁹*For God has destined us not for wrath but for obtaining salvation through our Lord Jesus Christ,* ¹⁰*who died for us, so that whether we are awake or asleep we may live with him.*

¹¹*Therefore encourage one another and build up each other, as indeed you are doing.*

1 Thessalonians 5:1–11

AN EXEGESIS OF 1 THESSALONIANS 5:1-11

Jerry L. Sumney

As we noted in connection with 1 Thessalonians 4, this letter is written to a young church. Paul had left them perhaps earlier than he might have hoped and so they seem to have some gaps in their understanding of the faith. Eschatology is among the things they do not understand clearly. Again, we should remember that everyone in the church believes that the church exists in the "Last Days." Now that nearly two decades have passed since the death and resurrection of Christ, believers have had to rethink what it means to say that they are living in the last days. They had clearly developed some strategies and some explanations for why the end had not come already. We will see some of those in 1 Thessalonians 5 (and we see others in Mark 13). As we saw in connection with 1 Thessalonians 4, the wider church had already dealt with deaths among believers, something that is new to the Thessalonian church. In 4:13–18 Paul has given them good news about those who have died and encouraged them to live the faith fully because they have such a future.

As chapter 5 begins, the broader subject remains eschatology, but the specific topic is now the *time* of the Parousia. Still, Paul has not lost sight of the Thessalonians' questions about whether or how those who have died participate in it. He begins by saying that he does not really need to write about this, but then does. He thinks he has taught them about it, but they still have questions or doubts.

Questions about the timing of the end are not surprising when we remember that these people are suffering persecution precisely because they are believers. They have left their civic and culturally acceptable gods and now worship only the God of Israel who raised Jesus from the dead. Their wider community and perhaps their families have responded to this change by turning against them. They are likely social pariahs and their economic status has worsened as people stop doing business with them. Given that their lives have gotten worse since they had begun to worship this God who was said to be the most powerful God there is, they want to know how that makes sense and how long it is going to last.

Early in the letter, Paul has reminded them that God's people often suffer at the hands of those who oppose God's will—that is, everyone who is not in the church (2:1–16). So they are not suffering as punishment from

God. Rather, those forces that control the world are trying to get them to give up their relationship with God. The apocalyptic outlook that we talked about in chapter 1 always sees the world governed by forces that oppose God's will. In 1 Thessalonians, Paul has drawn out one of the consequences of those evil powers controlling the economic, social, and political structures of the world: those on God's side are persecuted. Thus, Paul has given them assurances about why they are suffering; now in 5:1–11 he addresses the question of how long this will last.

As he did in 4:13–18, Paul sets out his basic response to the issue immediately after stating the question. For anyone who is inclined to calculate when the Day of the Lord will come, Paul's response is, it will come when you least expect it. Verse 2 may contain a bit of irony that is lost in most translations. The adverb translated "very well" (*akribōs*) in the NRSV is more literally "accurately," "precisely," or "exactly." So Paul says, "you yourselves know precisely that the Day of the Lord comes as a thief in the night." Just as it seems they know how to calculate precisely when the Day is to come, we find that what they know so exactly is that *they don't know*. The image of the thief in the night seems to be one of the ways the wider church had begun to talk about the second coming. Rather than emphasizing that it is coming soon, they have started saying it will come unexpectedly. The image of it coming as a thief in the night seems to have been widespread in the first generation of the church. It is found in Matthew (24:43), and in Luke (12:39), in 2 Peter (3:10), and Revelation (16:15). It appears, then, across a broad spectrum of branches of the church. This suggests that it is one of the earliest ways that the church began to think about what they saw as the delay of the return of Christ. Very early in the church's life they said it is impossible to know when the end is coming, it will simply be a surprise. This image allows them to maintain the certainty of the coming without that being dependent on knowing when it would come.

Verse 3 goes on to say that not only will the Parousia come when no one expects it, but it will also be sudden. Then Paul adds an ominous and emphatic[1] note: there is absolutely no escape! Its inescapability is as certain as labor is for a pregnant woman. Everyone will be caught up in the event. This is an important affirmation for those Thessalonian church members who are suffering persecution. This promises that their oppressors will not get away with what they are doing.

---

1. Paul uses two negative particles here, two words which mean "no," to make the point emphatic. A reasonable rendering would be, "they will by no means escape."

It is important to recognize that this warning is not given to church members, but to "them." This distinction between "them" and believers is made clear not only by the third person pronouns (they) in v. 3, but also by the direct contrast with "you" beginning in v. 4. Throughout vv. 3–8 this contrast is stark. There are the children of light and the day opposed to those of darkness and the night; there are church members and "the rest"; the sleeping and drunk on one hand and the awake and sober on the other. Such clear-cut separations between the people of God and the evil ones are common in apocalyptic texts. Given that the Thessalonians' experience of the world is one of alienation and opposition, these unmistakable distinctions show that apocalyptic comes from and speaks to those who know just what "Whoever is not with me is against me" (Matt 12:30) means. There are only two classifications for people within this framework: child of God and child of the devil. There are no other possibilities. Paul goes so far as to call outsiders, those who persecute the church, darkness and night, not just as the children of those dark forces. Having only these two conceptual categories makes sense of the early church's experience of persecution in a culture that explicitly supports other, contradictory values and uses all the types of powers that cultures have to enforce those values. In such settings, these drastic contrasts are completely understandable.

Verse 4 not only distinguishes believers from others, it says that the sudden and unpredictable coming of Christ in judgment should not catch them off their guard because they are children of the day and are not in darkness. If taken out of its context, someone might assert that this statement shows that the church will know when the Parousia is coming. But in its context, this is the opening statement in a series of exhortations to watchfulness and self-control. The unpredictably and suddenness of the Parousia becomes a reason for always living as one should because Christ may return at any time and without warning. It will not catch them off guard because they are constantly ready for it, not because they know when it is coming.

Beyond the knowledge that the moment of accountability before God may come at any moment, this text supports its exhortation to the moral life by giving the readers a place of high status by calling them children of God. It then calls on them to live up to that identity. This is sometimes called Paul's use of the indicative and the imperative, grammatical terms borrowed to express the relationship between what is and what must be done. Paul often explains who believers are or explicates some of the blessings they have through the grace of God (the indicative) and then uses those things directly as the bases for ethical demands (the imperative). It is like when my parents would remind me that I was a member of the Sumney family, and Sumneys act in a specific way. By this means, the reality of the new existence they have as believers in Christ who possess God's blessings becomes the basis for the ethical demands that are part of those blessings.

Paul uses the imagery of being children of the light or the dark and children of either the day or night to ground his exhortations about readiness. The day is the time of goodness, while the night is the time when people get drunk and fall asleep. By "fall asleep" Paul means to lapse into behavior that shows a person is not ready for the second coming and its judgment. Since believers are children of the day, they do not engage in those immoral behaviors and remain alert, not falling asleep.

Paul adds here that since the Thessalonians are children of God, God supplies them with the armor they need to retain self-control.[2] They are given the "breastplate of faith and love." We should remember here that when Paul speaks of faith, he does not refer to a set of beliefs. For Paul, faith includes a manner of life; it is faithfulness to a way of life that is consistent with who we know God to be in Christ. This piece of armor is particularly important when they face persecution. It enables them to both remain faithful and have love. It is not specified, but it seems probable that this love is the love they continue to have for fellow church members. Love for others is not excluded, but when a community faces pressure from outside it is easy for its members to turn on one another. The seriousness of the ethical demands being made on them may be reinforced by Paul's reference to the "hope of salvation," i.e., salvation remains future and contingent upon their watchfulness. However, immediately after the warning tone is sounded, Paul offers reassurance; they must be self-controlled because God has set them apart for salvation, not wrath. Thus, while their salvation is contingent on their behavior, it is dependent on the will and activity of God accomplished through Christ. It is God's intention to save them.

The relationship seen here (5:9) between God and Christ in the work of salvation is precisely the same as was already expressed in 4:14: salvation is an activity of God that is worked through Christ. What Paul has in mind by saying that this salvation is accomplished through Christ is seen in part in v. 10 where he identifies the death of Jesus as a death "for us." Paul does

---

2. This armor brings the Thessalonians the Pauline trio of faith, hope, and love, though in a different order.

not explain how this death functions for us, he adds only that it is through that death that we will live with Christ. This expression may well point to another way that salvation is accomplished through Christ. Both here and in 4:17 the final state of believers is "with the Lord/him." Thus, in some way, salvation is life with Christ.

Verse 10 also returns us to the concern that initiated the discussion of eschatological matters, the place of the dead. In 5:6–7 Paul used "awake" and "asleep" as metaphors for being ready or not being ready for the second coming and judgment. In 4:13 he had used "asleep" as a metaphor for being dead. In 5:10 he returns to using "asleep" to refer to death and "awake" to mean being alive. As he did in chapter 4, Paul again asserts that it does not matter whether believers live until the Parousia or die before it, their fate is the same, they will be with Christ.

Just as it does not matter whether one is alive or dead at the second coming, so Paul has said that it does not matter how long it takes the end to come. What is important is that a person always be ready because what seems like a delay does not signal that the eventual coming is less certain. Whenever it happens and whoever is alive or dead, believers can be certain that they will live with Christ. All New Testament authors point their readers away from speculations about timing and focus their attention on the certainty of God's act to render justice and reward the faithful.

The final verse of this section, 5:11, states again the overall goal of discussing eschatology: they are to use this material to encourage/exhort and build up one another. This was also given as the goal of the section ending at 4:18. *Parakaleō* is used in both 4:18 and 5:11. Sometimes this verb means to comfort or encourage, other times it means to exhort or urge someone to do something. It seems likely that both aspects of this word are being drawn on here: the comfort they derive from these reminders about the certainty of the future acts of God to make all things right is intended to spur them on to faithfulness. This is often a central goal of apocalyptic writings. The purpose of remembering the promise of God's future act is to move believers to live as God wants them to live now, to work for what God wants for the world now. Here in 1 Thessalonians, the readers are encouraged to be faithful in spite of opposition and persecution, knowing that God is faithful and loving and that God's purposes will not be thwarted in the end.

APOCALYPSE WHEN?

SERMON IDEAS FOR 1 THESSALONIANS 5:1-11

Leah D. Schade

Preaching 1 Thessalonians in the midst of anxiety

Whether or not members of a congregation are susceptible to doomsday prophecies or end-time predictions, the cultural artifacts around us stoke fear and sometimes even panic. As ridiculous as they seem, the bold-face headlines screaming about end-of-the-world prognostications from grocery check-out magazine racks are difficult to ignore. Similarly, religious leaders who peddle apocalyptic hysteria have a great deal to gain from convincing people to follow their instructions (and give money to their ministries) to prepare for Jesus' second coming.

Consider, for example, the way commercial apocalypticists have appropriated Paul's description of Jesus' second coming "like a thief" (v. 4). The 1972 Christian end-times movie *A Thief in the Night* was marketed as a thriller and boasted over 300 million viewers. According to Barbara Rossing in her book, *The Rapture Exposed: The Message of Hope in the Book of Revelation*, "The heroine 'disregards prophetic biblical warning and the truth begins to unfold. Can she escape the dramatic, haunting circumstances? Is there a way out? The climax is riveting!'"[3]

Despite the hijacking of Paul's words for commercial purposes, a congregation that is struggling with factors that are threatening their continuation as a church will likely resonate with the anxiety articulated in this passage. Dwindling numbers in the church's pews, bank account, or membership rolls do not engender feelings of confidence about the future. Likewise, a community that has suffered any kind of calamity due to weather-related catastrophes, racial/ethnic violence, or the slow march of shuttered factories and shops in an economic downturn will instinctively understand the kind of distress that the Thessalonian church experienced. This is why exegeting the context of this passage is important for the hearers.

---

3. Rossing, *The Rapture Exposed*, 20.

1 Thessalonians 5:1–11

How to be ready

Sumney stresses that the focus of Paul's words in chapter 5 of 1 Thessalonians is to urge the believers in the church to be prepared in the midst of uncertainty. Being alert, aware, and ready for what is certainly coming can have, ironically, a calming effect. Instead of frantically worrying and fretting, a congregation can direct their energy into doing the work that Paul calls us to do.

Sometimes churches are engaged in doing the work of God for so long, they forget the significance of what they are doing. The church pantry that has been serving the hungry for years. The Bible study group that has been faithfully meeting and ministering to each other for a decade. The quilting group that has sent hundreds of blankets and quilts to overseas missions for twenty years. All of these need a homiletical boost once in a while in order to frame them theologically and biblically as the ministries that prepare us for Christ's coming. They do so by creating the habitus of paying attention to those in need, attuning our hearts and minds to the word of God, and thinking beyond our own concerns about survival to see and reach out to our neighbors near and far.

The preacher can point to what it looks like to be "awake" by sharing examples of what they have observed in the ordinary practices of the congregation that give evidence of preparing for Christ's coming. Welcoming children to the church, advocating for justice, being active in a local effort to improve the lives of the community, visiting the sick and those unable to come to church—all of these are things church members do on a regular basis without fanfare. But they are, in fact, examples of preparing for Jesus. They are habits and practices that keep us aware and awake, enable us to share this life together as the church, and receive the coming of Christ with joy and certainty of God's grace.

Even if a congregation's end is certain (and all congregations close at some point), a preacher can encourage them to prepare themselves for Jesus with as much gusto as they can muster. What that preparation looks like will depend, of course, on the make-up of the membership. But it still behooves the preacher to urge a prophetic stretch for the faithful.

Apocalypse When?

"PAYING ATTENTION TO WHAT REALLY MATTERS"

A Sermon on 1 Thessalonians 5:1–11

Leah D. Schade

(I preached this sermon in 2011 at Spirit and Truth Worship Center, a small urban church in Yeadon, Pennsylvania, part of the Philadelphia metropolitan area. The congregation was made up of members of African descent who, at the time, were struggling to keep their congregation afloat in the midst of serious challenges with their church building. Yet they continued to welcome new members, including children from the neighborhood who participated in the church's youth group. The story of doomsday evangelist Harold Camping's failed prophecy predicting the arrival of Jesus' second coming was the subject of much discussion earlier that year.)

There they were—the faithful followers eagerly awaiting the second coming of Christ. They stood gawking up at the sky with a calendar in one hand and a stopwatch in the other. They were giddy with an excitement that had spread far and wide. Surely, the time was almost upon them; the end was almost here!

Am I talking about the Christians in the early church expecting Jesus' second coming? No! I'm talking about the followers of Harold Camping who had convinced thousands of people that May 21, 2011, would be the end of the world as we know it.

Family Radio Network, the company that sponsored Camping, had a huge countdown clock on their website. They spent millions of dollars advertising about the end of the world. No matter that the eighty-nine-year-old man had been wrong before when his 1994 end-times prediction failed. This time he was sure he had gotten it right. And the hype was unbelievable.

Finally, the hour arrived, 6 PM on May 21. It came . . . and it went. No earthquakes rumbled across the planet. No fire fell from the sky. The Earth kept on spinning as it has done for billions of years. One of Camping's devoted followers stood in the middle of New York City's Times Square nearly speechless. After having spent his own money to put up advertising about the end of the world, he was beset with confusion and disbelief. "I can't tell you what I feel right now . . . I don't understand it. I don't know. I don't understand what happened. Obviously, I haven't understood it correctly because we're still here," he said.[4]

Well, he's in good company. Because Jesus himself said he didn't know when the end of the world would occur. "But about that day and hour no one knows, neither the angels of heaven, nor the Son, but only the Father" (Matt 24:36). And Paul was clear with the Christians in Thessalonica that they could not predict the day and time of Christ's coming. "Now concerning the times and the seasons, brothers and sisters, you do not need to have anything written to you. For you yourselves know very well that the day of the Lord will come like a thief in the night" (1 Thess 5:1-2).

Yet Harold Camping, like so many apocalyptic fanatics before him, was so sure. And he was so wrong.

Truth be told, many of us secretly breathed a little sigh of relief on May 22. I called a friend of mine that day and said jokingly, "Oh, I'm so disappointed to get hold of you. I thought for sure you'd have been taken up in the Rapture by now." And we had a good laugh.

But then we soberly reflected on a deeper truth. The world actually *did* come to an end for tens of thousands of people on May 21, 2011. In fact, 70,000 people died that day. That's approximately how many people die every day on the Earth. Of course, death is a natural part of life. But what is distressing is how many of those deaths were due to human cruelty and systemic evil. In fact, 7,000 of the people who died on May 21 suffered from entirely preventable maladies such as malaria, water-borne illnesses, infections, and hunger—all in the poorest places on earth. People in those areas don't get hyped up about global cataclysmic catastrophes. The end of the world has already swept through their villages, lives, and bodies, with or without Harold Camping's predictions.

The real sin is just how much money was spent on this end-times campaign for absolutely no reason. "Family Radio spent millions on more than 5,000 billboards and 20 RVs plastered with the doomsday message. In 2009, the nonprofit reported in IRS filings that it received $18.3 million in donations and had assets of more than $104 million, including $34 million in stocks or other publicly traded securities."[5]

I know their motivation was to save souls for Jesus. But if you really want to save souls, you need to spend that money on saving their bodies first. All those millions of dollars could have been invested in the things

---

4. McKinley, "The only rapture was in the anticipation."
5. McKinley, "The only rapture was in the anticipation."

that Jesus *does* call us to do: feed the hungry, clothe the naked, visit the sick and imprisoned, and help those who are most vulnerable. Paul says, "since we belong to the day, let us be sober, and put on the breastplate of faith and love, and for a helmet the hope of salvation" (1 Thess 5:8). Paul isn't just talking about faith as a set of beliefs. Faith is how we live, how we act toward others, how we minister to those in need, how we are church together in the midst of a cruel and dangerous world.

At the same time, we have to acknowledge the existential threats to our planet. An end is coming to the way of life as we know it. Islands and coastlines are disappearing because of melting arctic ice and sea level rise. Species are going extinct right before our eyes. Extreme weather events are wreaking havoc on communities. So many people are killed by gun violence within our city. People are indeed scared, and with good reason. Always the next terrorist attack or military offensive looms on the horizon. Always the next act of police violence against persons of color threatens the community.

On a more personal level, at some point, the world as you know it *is* going to come to an end, whether through illness, loss of a job, the end of a marriage, death of friend, spouse, or child, or, finally, your own death. Sometimes there's no rhyme or reason. The end just comes. Like a thief in the night.

This is why Paul wrote this letter to the Christians in Thessalonica, to give them instructions on how to be ready for Jesus' ultimate return. The Thessalonians were deeply troubled by the persecution they suffered as a church in the first century. Society rejected them, family and friends shut them out, and some of them were killed for their beliefs. They wondered when—or if—Christ would return, or whether their suffering for the faith was in vain.

While most Christians in this country don't have to endure harassment for their faith, many in this congregation know what it's like to face discrimination and prejudice, to have the door slammed in your face, to be rejected or punished because of the color of your skin. And while this church hasn't been threatened with persecution, we can certainly relate to the Thessalonians' feelings of anxiety about whether or not we can hold on. An old, broken-down furnace, asbestos to remove, and mold in the basement are serious issues when a church's budget is stretched to the breaking point.

1 Thessalonians 5:1-11

But Paul is clear: just because we cannot, and should not, try to predict the day and the hour, we still must live our lives by being ready for Christ's return. Like the contractions that come for the pregnant woman, when the water breaks, there's no stopping what's to come. So Paul tells us that we must live our lives in a constant state of readiness for Jesus. We are to be "children of the day" (v. 4). This means we must live as God calls us to live, which means following the commandments, ministering to those in need, and preparing ourselves to be ready when Christ appears.

Yet, people like Harold Camping and advertising executives create so much hysteria, some people go from having a healthy concern about the future to reacting with fear about what might happen. This is where our culture and the consumer machine around us see an opportunity to manipulate those who are afraid. Doomsday peddlers are reaping an incredible amount of wealth from our intangible feelings of worry and dread. They have a great deal of money to make from our feelings of inadequacy, our fears, and our insatiable desires for more. Camping convinced his followers to give him their money to secure their place with God. Our capitalist society convinces its followers to spend their money and acquire material goods with the false hope of securing their future and keeping the end away.

They are profiting from our fears and anxieties because we have forgotten a key aspect of Paul's teaching: "keep awake." The Greek word is *grēgoriō* and it means to keep watch, to pay attention, to wake up. How do we do that?

Our Buddhist friends have a word for this wakefulness, this state of attentiveness: *sati*. It means "mindfulness." It means being in the moment, attending to your life, keeping your attention on the people and tasks before you. It means putting aside those things that are trying to dull or distract our brains from paying attention.

But as Christians, our mindfulness takes on a different quality. Because of Christ's claim upon our lives, we pay attention to people who are suffering. It's about waking up to the ways in which systemic sin has taken over our institutions, our ways of doing business, our education systems, even our churches. And once we've woken up, we call out those sins such as white privilege, pollution, violence, economic oppression.

Paul's words remind us that we have an opportunity to live our lives differently. Instead of all of this doomsday distraction that keeps us from being honest about our fears, we can respond with a trust that by caring for others, by caring for our world, we will truly be prepared to meet Jesus. In caring for the least of these, we will build a community that is filled with hope and joy instead of fear and dread.

Paul is compelling us to prepare for Christ's return not with doomsday clocks but through the work of justice. It's about cultivating relationships, working with people both within the church and beyond our walls to advocate for equity. For the rights of the oppressed. For the restoration of healthy water, land, and air. I see this happening in our own congregation where we serve our neighbors through our youth group, through our advocacy for clean air, and through our ministry to local children in need. Not to mention our Bible studies that help people build a living faith.

This is the kind of apocalyptic waiting I want to do; it's an active waiting that gets us busy with our hands and feet instead standing still, looking skyward. When I do that, I am much less afraid of the end. I am filled with joy of the Holy Spirit because we are doing as Paul says, encouraging one another and building each other up.

I don't care whether it's Harold Camping or a co-worker, a family member or your next-door neighbor who tells you that the world is coming to an end. When we hear those warnings about impending doom, we can say: help us pay attention, Lord. Show us how we can prepare for your coming. Show us how we can praise you. Show us how we can serve your people. Show us how we can be filled with the Holy Spirit in joyful anticipation of your return. Amen.

Chapter 10

Revelation 14:1–13

¹*Then I looked, and there was the Lamb, standing on Mount Zion! And with him were one hundred forty-four thousand who had his name and his Father's name written on their foreheads.* ²*And I heard a voice from heaven like the sound of many waters and like the sound of loud thunder; the voice I heard was like the sound of harpists playing on their harps,* ³*and they sing a new song before the throne and before the four living creatures and before the elders. No one could learn that song except the one hundred forty-four thousand who have been redeemed from the earth.* ⁴*It is these who have not defiled themselves with women, for they are virgins; these follow the Lamb wherever he goes. They have been redeemed from humankind as first fruits for God and the Lamb,* ⁵*and in their mouth no lie was found; they are blameless.*

⁶*Then I saw another angel flying in midheaven, with an eternal gospel to proclaim to those who live on the earth—to every nation and tribe and language and people.* ⁷*He said in a loud voice, "Fear God and give him glory, for the hour of his judgment has come; and worship him who made heaven and earth, the sea and the springs of water."* ⁸*Then another angel, a second, followed, saying, "Fallen, fallen is Babylon the great! She has made all nations drink of the wine of the wrath of her fornication."* ⁹*Then another angel, a third, followed them, crying with a loud voice, "Those who worship the beast and its image, and receive a mark on their foreheads or on their hands,* ¹⁰*they will also drink the wine of God's wrath, poured unmixed into the cup of his anger, and they will be tormented with fire and sulfur in the presence of the holy angels and in the presence*

of the Lamb. ¹¹*And the smoke of their torment goes up forever and ever. There is no rest day or night for those who worship the beast and its image and for anyone who receives the mark of its name."* ¹²*Here is a call for the endurance of the saints, those who keep the commandments of God and hold fast to the faith of Jesus.*

¹³*And I heard a voice from heaven saying, "Write this: Blessed are the dead who from now on die in the Lord." "Yes," says the Spirit, "they will rest from their labors, for their deeds follow them."*

INTRODUCTION TO REVELATION

JERRY L. SUMNEY

The book of Revelation has been one of the most popular and one of the most frightening books in the canon. It has spoken to many groups and has been understood in very different ways. It is important for us, then, to locate this document in its own time and to try to understand its message in that context. We begin with what we can know about the historical setting of the writing as a whole.

Revelation is written by John, a Jewish-Christian prophet who was familiar with the congregations of western Asia Minor (today's Turkey). The text provides no evidence that points to the Apostle John as the author. This writer's authority did not come from a claim to apostolic office, but from the recipients' knowledge of him as a prophet and from the medium of the writing, an account of a revelation from God.

Revelation was written in a time of persecution. The letters to the seven churches at the beginning of this work describe various kinds of persecution. Because of this, Revelation is usually dated late in the reign of Domitian (81–96 CE). It is often asserted that there was a severe persecution of Christians during this time and that Revelation is a response to that persecution. However, there is almost no evidence outside Revelation that there was a systematic, empire-wide persecution of Christians during this time.

Still, there were local bursts of it, as the death of James and the need for Peter to escape Jerusalem show (Acts 12:1–19). Paul had also been persecuted by local magistrates (2 Cor 11:23–24; Acts 16:16–40). This means that the persecution the churches in western Turkey were enduring could have been inflicted earlier than the nineties. Even without broad governmental and violent persecution, Christians faced many things they interpreted as persecution and as the work of Satan. John clearly identifies Rome as the primary embodiment of the powers of evil and the source of persecution. This suggests that it comes from a time after the Empire had begun to sponsor persecution, often in the form of demanding offering incense to the emperor, a violation of the commandment against idolatry. John is clear that Rome is God's enemy and that God's victory will destroy Rome

Most persecution of church members in the first century was social and economic, rather than state-sponsored threats. This sort of persecution should not be seen as trivial or as less difficult to endure than our usual conception of persecution as something that involves physical torture or death. This latter kind of persecution is brutal and painful, but swift. Persecution in the form of economic disadvantaging and being treated as a social outcast is something that must be endured constantly. It is not just a matter of standing bravely for your faith one time, but of having to question your commitment to Christ in the face of continual difficulty and pain inflicted on both yourself and your family. Most early Christians were from among the lower reaches of society, a society in which there was almost no middle class. Most of these people had little or no disposable income. After their conversions to Christianity, things probably got worse for them. After all, becoming a Christian meant that they were expected to give up certain activities that brought economic advantage.

For example, losing business contacts for day laborers or small business owners could be the difference between steady income and going hungry. Still, John calls on them not to go their trade guild meetings where the meal included food that was sacrificed to the god of that trade (2:19–20). These meetings were places where business was discussed and deals were made. If you suddenly refuse to attend, you lose all you might have gained there, and when you explained why you weren't there it would often mean that those who did attend stopped doing business with you. But in addition to these pressures, when Revelation is written some are being pressured to confess that Caesar is Lord (3:8) and some faced imprisonment and death (2:9–10, 13). John, the author of the book, has himself been exiled to the island of Patmos and his letter to Pergamum mentions a member of their church who had been martyred (2:13).

Whether the persecution was from Domitian or from some more common experiences, the perception of the first readers of Revelation was that the world was against them. Their experience of reality made it seem painfully obvious that Satan was in control and making things difficult for them. This is the kind of experience that often produced apocalyptic texts. The struggling readers need a word of hope about the victory of God and about their participation in it. If we remember that the earliest believers in Christ believed that the End was very near,[1] the difficulties these readers faced are made all the more severe. Sixty years have passed since the church first began to proclaim that the second coming was near. Belief that the End was coming may have begun to wane for some. If so, then there is no prospect of relief from the difficult circumstances in which they live. Revelation renews that hope, saying that the End is near, even if not as soon as most had thought. Thus, they are exhorted to remain faithful and detached from the world and its temporary advantages.

The primary purposes of Revelation, then, are: 1) to assure those who are suffering that God will set things right; 2) to assure them that God will do this soon, and 3) to exhort them to faithfulness, given the certainty and swiftness of this action by God. All the strange (to us) imagery and numbers in the book contribute to those purposes. The imagery was not intended to be literal or difficult. Revelation 17:1–14 is a clear demonstration that the symbols are not to be understood literally. In this text John interprets the image he describes, which gives us a key to how to read other material in the book. In this passage, John describes a scarlet beast and a great prostitute, which he identifies as the Roman Empire. His images refer to things his first readers know about. The imagery of this book is focused on people and events of the first century. John did not plot out the events of the world's distant future. Rather, he spoke about people and events the first readers could easily identify. As with all apocalyptic, he had to do this in veiled language, but within the traditional imagery of this genre, his references were clear enough to his original readers. If Revelation was to be helpful to its recipients, it had to speak to their time. It would do little to bolster their endurance to tell them that they should remain faithful and hopeful in these difficult times because God would act decisively on their behalf—in about 2,000 years! As with all apocalyptic writers, John assures the readers that God will act soon (1:1; 6:9–11; 22:20). Thus, Revelation can

---

1. E.g., 1 Thessalonians was written because these Christians did not know how to understand deaths within their congregation. They had believed that the second coming would occur before anyone in their church died.

never be used to predict when the End will come because it envisions only characters and events of the first century.

The cyclical patterns that shape the story line of Revelation also show that it cannot be used to plot out the future or our times. The book does not produce a chronological sequence of events which lead to the End. Instead, it often describes the consequences of disobeying God, looking at those consequences from different perspectives. The seven seals of chapters 6–8 are a good example. The first four of these seals reveal what happens in the areas of politics, war, and economics when people disobey God. It is not the order of these things that is important, but that they are all consequences of not living as God would have humans live. In the larger scheme, if Revelation gave the blueprint for the world's future, chapter 11 would be the end of the book. At the end of chapter 11 the day of judgment has arrived and "The kingdom of the world has become the kingdom of our Lord and of his Messiah" (v. 15). This concludes all of world history, the victory of God is secured, the righteous are rewarded, and the wicked are punished (vv. 16–18). But, of course, the book does not end here; chapter 12 begins another cycle within the book. The point here is that Revelation does not intend to do what it is often used to do, i.e., to predict the course of events in the world so that we can predict the day of the End. The reason we cannot predict world history from Revelation is not that we do not understand it well enough, but that it never intended to enable its readers to make such predictions in the first place.

The message of Revelation is something far more important than any delineation of the sequence of events that lead to the End. It proclaims that whatever those events are, you can be certain that God will be victorious. It assures readers of God's love and care for them in spite of the suffering they are enduring. It promises that the life God has in store for the faithful will more than make up for the suffering they are enduring in the present. It reminds readers that if they remain faithful, they will live with God in that victory over evil. The exhortation to faithfulness also includes the warning that failing to maintain their faith will mean that they will be excluded from this glorious future. Thus, John does not divert their attention from the present world. Instead, he calls them to do God's will despite the cost that way of life exacts. Even as he reminds them that they will not escape persecution by the Empire, he says that his vision is a call for patience and faithfulness (13:10). His vision assures them that God, not the Empire, has the last word. He reminds them that it is through their faithfulness to God that they will participate in God's victory over evil and in the blessed life God gives the faithful.

Revelation 14:1–13

AN EXEGESIS OF REVELATION 14

Jerry L. Sumney

As we noted above, the first half of Revelation concluded with the end of chapter 11, where the kingdom of God is established and the day of judgment has come. Instead of ending there, John begins a new set of visions that cover the same period of time as the previous larger cycle but provide a different viewpoint on some things and encourage faithfulness among his readers.[2] The new start at chapter 12 begins with a "great sign" and chapter 14 concludes the first cycle of visions in this second major section of visions. While the details of the visions in chapters 12—13 are sometimes obscure and difficult, it seems clear by the end of chapter 13 that the primary evil being characterized is the emperor cult. Inhabitants of many cities were required to offer incense to the genius of the emperor at this time. Deification of the emperor had developed to the point that Domitian was even requiring people to address him as "our lord and god."

Chapter 13 concludes by speaking of the emperor cult as the beast whose number is 666, a number that is further identified as a "human number" (v. 18). Calling it a "human number" means that it represents someone's name. Using numerology (assigning letters of the alphabet a numerical value—a well-known practice in the ancient Mediterranean world), the identity of this person is intended to be fairly easy for John's readers to discern. Most critical interpreters agree that the person referred to with this number is Nero. But even that name is symbolic, representing the emperor, because Nero was probably already dead when Revelation was written. So it is the emperor and the emperor cult that are identified as the enemy of the people of God at the end of chapter 13.

Chapter 14 begins with a break in the action, which has been constant and violent since the beginning of chapter 12. Such breaks are common in Revelation. Chapter 14:1–5 provides a glimpse into heaven and of the Lamb on Mt. Zion. With the Lamb are 144,000 who have on their foreheads the names of the Lamb and of God. This seal indicates that they have been faithful to God (see Ezek 9) and that they now belong to God as God's own possession. Their identity as God's own possession is reinforced by John

---

2. For a good brief examination of Revelation that uses this outline see Metzger, *Breaking the Code*.

saying that they have been bought (redeemed) from among humanity to be God's and the Lamb's (v. 4).

The number 144,000 is symbolic. It is derived from two complete numbers, 12 and 10 (12 x 12 x 10 x 10—in chapter 7, there are 12,000 from each of the twelve tribes). Twelve was, of course, also the number of tribes in Israel. Thus, it symbolizes the complete number of this group. The 10 x 10 intends to show that this vision pictures a huge and a complete multitude.

These 144,000 are the antithesis of those who have the mark of the beast (13:16–17). John identifies them as the firstfruits for God and the Lamb and those who follow the Lamb wherever he goes. These characteristics probably indicate that the 144,000 are martyrs because they are willing to follow the Lamb even to death and are the first sample of the whole people of God who are now being encouraged to remain faithful as they see the position that previous martyrs occupy. The large number of martyrs indicates that the contest between God and the powers of evil is a mighty struggle. As the firstfruits they are also a pledge that the rest of the harvest will be successful. Having 144,000 in this group implies that the full number of martyrs must be completed before the end comes and it implies that these faithful will be victorious.

Those in this group are also said to have not "defiled themselves with women," to be free from lying, and to be blameless. The first of these characteristics may indicate that John valued lifelong celibacy and thus advocated a somewhat ascetic ideal. While this possibility is more probable than is usually acknowledged, the sexual purity mentioned here may be metaphorical. Adultery is nearly always symbolic in Revelation: it stands for idolatry. John probably took this metaphor from the prophets of the Hebrew Bible who often used it to speak of Israel going after other gods. If this metaphorical interpretation is correct, then the contrast between these faithful 144,000 and those sealed with the mark of the beast is yet more emphatic. Furthermore, it may be that the lie that is not found in their mouths is that of denying their faith in face of persecution.

These 144,000 are probably also the ones who are singing the "new song" before God. Though John does not reveal the content of this song, we should probably view it as a song of praise and victory similar to those seen elsewhere in Revelation and perhaps even drawing on the songs of victory the Israelites sang on the other side of the sea after God saved them from the Egyptians (Exod 15:1–21).

Revelation 14:1–13

The vision of the joyous, victorious martyrs worshiping before God leads to a vision of a sequence of angels each of whom proclaims the arrival of the judgment of God (vv. 6ff.). This message of the arrival of God's judgment is called gospel in v. 6. The long-awaited expression of the justice of God is good news for John and his readers. Though this may seem harsh to us, God's justice is essential if we are going to be able to trust God. God must do what is right and just because God must remain faithful to God's own character. The good news of the justice of God includes judgment in which God punishes evil and rewards righteousness. This first message of good news may also allow for repentance since the hearers are called to fear God and to worship God.

The second angel proclaims the fall of Babylon (that is, Rome) which will be described in more detail later in chapters 17–18. The third angel specifies the criteria for judgment: participation in the emperor cult and perhaps in other aspects of the pagan culture that John thinks are inappropriate for people who profess faith in God. This angel also describes the punishment of those who engage in the condemned activities. The point of this is not only to see the Christians' enemies suffer, but also to call the readers to faithfulness when they see what happens to those without faith. This point is made explicit in the following sentence, "Here is a call for the endurance of the saints" (v. 12). Verse 13 explains why this announcement of judgment and description of the punishment of the wicked can encourage faithfulness. Here John is told to write that those who die in the Lord are blessed, to which the Spirit adds that they will rest from their labors. This, then, is the other side of the judgment—the blessing of the faithful.

Verses 14–20 contain another description of God's judgment on the wicked. In v. 14 John sees one who is "like a son of man" seated on a cloud with a crown on his head and a sickle in his hand. "Son of man" is, of course, the title Jesus usually uses for himself in the Synoptic Gospels. Coming from Daniel 7, this description of a heavenly figure seems related to eschatological expectations but remains vague. While it is possible that "one like a son of man" designates Christ as the one on the cloud, v. 15 mentions "another angel" and also seems to identify the "one like a son of man" as an angel. We might also note that this "one like a son of man" takes orders from an angel. It seems unlikely that John would have Christ take orders from an angel. Further telling against identifying this figure with Christ is that yet another angel appears in v. 17 with a sickle and performs the same task as the one on the cloud a second time.

The image of reaping with a sickle to signify God's judgment comes from Joel 3:11–16 (esp. v. 13), where Joel summons the nations which surround and trouble Israel to the valley of decision. There they are to be reaped and tread upon in the wine press that overflows with their wickedness. John expands this image to worldwide proportions, a move nearly made by Joel who spoke of the sun and moon being darkened and the stars retreating at the judgment of God. John's expansion of this image has God's judgment exercised on the whole world rather than having God's judgment of a part of the world produce cosmic repercussions. Since this imagery of reaping is associated with condemnatory judgment in Joel, the two reapings in Revelation 14:14–20 probably both refer to a reaping of the wicked, even though it seems repetitious. Perhaps the first reaping is an initial judgment of God, similar to those in the first half of the book which were intended in part to lead to repentance (e.g. 9:20–21), which is followed by the final judgment.

After the reapings are completed, what these beings have reaped is put into the "winepress of the wrath of God." In addition to drawing on Joel 3, John may also echo Isaiah 63:16, where God as warrior returns from crushing Edom (a symbol of the enemies of God's people) under his feet in the winepress. The divine warrior in the Isaiah passage says that he alone defeated Edom and that it was his wrath that sustained him in the battle. The imagery, then, is not new nor is the idea that God's wrath has a part in judgment. However, God's wrath should not be understood as unbridled anger that outstrips what is appropriate. Rather, God's wrath is the just, fair reaction of a righteous God who has seen the creation abused and God's own people injured. What God's wrath delivers is just punishment, the actions which must be meted out if God is to be a God of justice, power, and love. Such judgment is not optional and it is not cruelty. Without judgment, which includes both condemnation and blessing, God cannot remain God, cannot remain true to Godself. Without just judgment, God cannot be trusted or worshiped. Thus, this punishment of the wicked is a divine necessity, a necessity for which we, with John, should be grateful.

Still, the description of this judgment is gruesome, with blood flowing as deep as a horse's bridle for 200 miles. This terrible sight intends to show the magnitude of the wickedness God is punishing and the thoroughness of God's justice at the end. The horrific impression this passage makes on us may well have been experienced differently by John's original readers. They knew the pain of persecution, whether it was social and economic alone or included physical violence. Their oppression called for a powerful response from God, which proclaimed that God understood the depths of their suffering and that God would not allow such injustice to be the final word. It is important to notice here that this battle against the wicked at judgment is carried out by God alone. The saints will not be loosed to do vengeance with injustice. No! This is a word about the justice and power of God, the God who hates oppression and injustice and the suffering of the righteous. This is also a word about the love God has for God's people; God will enter into judgment to make things just for them. The purpose of this judgment, then, is to make things just for the righteous and the wicked and to allow God to remain the God who is worthy of praise and worship. As hard of a passage as this is to hear, "Here is a call for the endurance of the saints."

Chapter 14 is another good example of the cyclical nature of the visions of Revelation. Once the judgment has been accomplished at the end of this chapter, a new series of actions begins: another portent and seven bowls. These bowls expand the compressed actions seen in chapter 14 and will lead to the final descriptions of God's judgment and the establishment of the kingdom of God. One emphasis of the cycle composed of chapters 12–14 is endurance of persecution. In 13:10 and 14:12 John writes that these visions are a call to endurance. These are the only two uses of this word (*hupomonê*) in Revelation after the letters to the seven churches (chs. 2—3). So, these initial proclamations of the second large vision cycle of Revelation (chs. 12–21) make the point of John's visions of God's judgment and of the blessed end of the faithful explicit. His point is to encourage the readers to maintain their faith in the midst of persecution. They are assured that the God to whom they are being faithful can and will act in accordance with the character of God—with love, power, and justice.

APOCALYPSE WHEN?

IDEAS FOR PREACHING ON REVELATION 14

Leah D. Schade

Preachers who follow the Revised Common Lectionary will not find any passage from Revelation 14 in the three-year cycle. However, the symbols and imagery from this particular chapter crystalize motifs in the book of Revelation that have found their way into popular culture and political discourse. Therefore, preachers may want to consider preaching on this chapter of Revelation as a single sermon or as part of a larger a sermon series on the entire book. (See chapters 11 and 12 for ideas for preaching on Revelation Chapters 21 and 22.)

Rapture theology, politics, and the public square

Understanding the recent history of the influence of Rapture theology on US politics and public discourse is important when preaching on Revelation, or any apocalyptic text for that matter. In the 1980s, President Ronald Reagan speculated that the violence in the Middle East was an indication that biblical prophecy was coming to fulfillment. In the 1990s, after the first *Left Behind* book was published, prophecy groups sprung up that encouraged members to see correlations between world events and the biblical "timeline" for the end times. In the 2000s, President George W. Bush, a born-again Christian, invoked apocalyptic language in the lead-up to the Iraq War. Among his cabinet members were fundamentalist Christians whose beliefs shaped US foreign policy in the Middle East. And when peace negotiations between Israel and Palestine were underway, high-profile evangelical leaders such as Pat Robertson, Jerry Falwell, and Tim LaHaye opposed these efforts because they believed such efforts would delay the beginning of Armageddon and the subsequent second coming of Christ.

As we write this book, the Trump administration is filled with evangelicals who attend weekly Bible studies led by Ralph Drollinger, director of the conservative right-wing organization, Capitol Ministries. Trump's Vice President Mike Pence is a staunch conservative Christian, and the Secretary of State Mike Pompeo has unashamedly confessed that his evangelical Christian beliefs influence his diplomacy.[3] While we are writing this chap-

---

3. Wong, "The Rapture and the Real World." Borger, "'Brought to Jesus.'"

ter in early 2020, evangelicals are cheering for Trump's attack on Iran, believing that a war with an enemy of Israel is key to setting up the conditions wherein the Rapture will begin.

Barbara Rossing describes the fundamentalist position this way: "The dispensationalist version of the biblical story line requires tribulation and war in the Middle East, not peace plans. That is the most terrifying aspect of the distorted theology." Rossing asserts, and we concur, that this is "the very reason why we cannot afford to give in to the dispensationalist version of the biblical story line—because real people's lives are at stake."[4] With this in mind, the preacher can help the congregation unpack the imagery and symbolism of Revelation 14 in order to gain historical perspective and properly situate it as a book of faith rather than as a crystal ball of prophecy foretelling doom and divine destruction.

The apocalyptic journey—follow the Lamb

Barbara Rossing describes John of Patmos's vision as an "apocalyptic journey" to which the faithful are invited in order to experience the power, justice, and love of God. But embarking on this journey means relinquishing a literalist reading of the text in order to hear its poetry. "As Kathleen Norris argues in her commentary on Revelation, 'this is a poet's book, which is probably the best argument for reclaiming it from fundamentalists. It doesn't tell, it shows, over and over again, its images unfolding, pushing hard against the limits of language and metaphor, engaging the listener in a tale that has the satisfying yet unsettling logic of a dream.'"[5]

This dream, ironically, compels us to wake up to the reality that is around us but is not immediately visible. At first, this vision may seem to be a terrifying predictor of global catastrophe. But the scenes of destruction and bizarre imagery are meant to alert us to the nature of Rome's and any other hegemonic system's oppressive empire. "Revelation's primary purpose is life-changing; it does not predict literal events," Rossing explains. "The book's goal is to exhort us to faithfulness to God by means of a new vision."[6]

The preacher will want to point out that these disturbing scenarios in Revelation are shown to John (and us) "precisely because there *is* still hope for us and for the earth. Indeed, the hope of the book of Revelation is that

---

4. Rossing, *The Rapture Exposed*, 46.
5. Rossing, *The Rapture Exposed*, 96.
6. Rossing, *The Rapture Exposed*, 96.

God's Lamb, Jesus, is already victorious and that God's people will be faithful to the Bible's vision of life."[7] In the exegesis above, Sumney explains that the symbolism of the number 144,000 represents the completeness of those who are "the firstfruits for God and the Lamb and those who follow the Lamb wherever he goes." Rossing suggests that following the Lamb means "renouncing all the seductions of imperial injustice and violence, so the threat of the plagues will be averted."[8]

The preacher might suggest that the congregation consider what it means to follow Jesus—even to martyrdom. While few individuals or congregations in the US will have experienced the kind of persecution that requires a martyr's death, the sermon can lift up examples of those whose faith in Jesus led them to service, even at risk of their own lives. What does it mean to follow the Lamb by accepting disadvantage for the sake of others?

Consider the example of a story shared with me about a medical doctor who traveled to western Africa to help stop the Ebola outbreak in 2014. He himself contracted the virus and almost died from the disease. Fortunately, he was flown back to the US and survived after emergency treatment. This man was willing to offer his assistance knowing full well the risk involved, even if it meant his life was in danger. And he did this because his faith compelled him to care for those in need.

This is not to imply that the congregation is necessarily expected to die for their faith. But the message of Revelation is "a call for the endurance of the saints, those who keep the commandments of God and hold fast to the faith of Jesus" (v. 12). The faithful are called to renounce the temptations of empire, live holy and righteous lives, work for the causes of justice, and be willing to sacrifice for the sake of serving those whom God loves, especially those who are vulnerable.

Such sacrifice can be done individually or, better yet, can be undertaken by the congregation as a whole. For example, congregations committed to church planting in order to start new ministries in underserved areas are willing to give of their membership, funds, and leadership. Congregations with a mission to lift up new leaders will establish scholarships, provide training and mentoring, and send out those they have raised up for the good of the larger church. Sacrifice involves giving time, money, space, and human resources in order to "hold fast to the faith of Jesus."

---

7. Rossing, *The Rapture Exposed*, 96.
8. Rossing, *The Rapture Exposed*, 96.

Revelation 14:1–13

Singing a new song

Most readers of Revelation will likely find the gruesome images of chapter 14 to be disturbing and perhaps even problematic. The notion of Jesus and the angels overseeing eternal torment of God's enemies is antithetical to our notions of God's unconditional love and mercy. Sumney notes that such imagery is meant to emphasize that those who oppose God and oppress the faithful will be held responsible. This is good news to those who have suffered under the reign of powerful forces that exploit, abuse, and oppress individuals and communities. However, such imagery could be interpreted by those very powers to further political, economic, and theocratic agendas intent on violence.

For example, in the best-selling book *Left Behind*, a character named Rayford celebrates the violence and blood of the "tribulation" wrought under the anti-Christ.[9] Earthquakes, fires, war, and natural disasters are, for Rapture-believers, proof of God bringing the predictions of Revelation to fruition. It is a sickening, twisted, and distorted theology that wants God to bring about death and destruction rather than the peace of the Lamb.

The preacher will need to be cognizant of the fact that such interpretations of Revelation are found not just among fringe groups but are, in fact, guiding the foreign and domestic policy decisions of lawmakers who ascribe to millennialism, as noted above. The preacher may want to raise this point in the sermon so as to contextualize the gravity and consequences of misinterpreting this text. At the same time, Ronald J. Allen suggests that preachers emphasize the hope in Revelation 14, noting "the fact that some people are still not resigned to empire, but hope and work for change."[10]

This hope is symbolized most beautifully in the description of the sound of music in the midst of the travail. An ethereal harp-like chorus assures John that "those still in the clutches of the Enemy may not yet experience it, but the decisive battle has already been won. The struggle continues, but the issue is no longer in doubt . . . This is the rock on which we stand: the absolute certainty of the triumph of God in the World," as Walter Wink explains.[11]

One hymn that draws on this imagery of the faithful gathered in the presence of God is "For All the Saints" by William Walsham How. This

---

9. LaHaye and Jenkins, *Left Behind*.
10. Allen, *I Will Tell You the Mystery*, 136.
11. Wink, *Engaging the Powers*, 321.

hymn is traditionally sung on All Saints Sunday, so the preacher could choose a passage from Revelation 14 as the text for the sermon that day. Celebrating the life of those who have died in faith, even as we continue our journey on earth, mirrors the celebration that arises in the midst of the conflict of Revelation. Wink notes that the placement of this victory song is intentional. "That is why the celebration of the divine victory does not take place at the end of the Book of Revelation, after the struggle is over. Rather, it breaks out all along the way," including here in 14:1–8. The faithful are "*enjoying* the struggle because it confirms their freedom. Even in the midst of conflict, suffering, or imprisonment, suddenly a hymn pierces the gloom, the heavenly hosts thunder in a mighty chorus, and our hearts grow lighter."[12]

---

12. Wink, *Engaging the Powers*, 321.

Revelation 14:1–13

"COMMEMORATING THE EARTH MARTYRS"

A Sermon on Revelation 14:1–13

Leah D. Schade

(A growing number of churches are holding Creation-centered worship services to celebrate Earth Day in April. This sermon is written for an Earth Day worship service and focuses on those who, like the martyrs in Revelation, lost their lives in serving God, God's people, and God's Creation.)

Today we are celebrating Earth Day. Preachers in many churches are extolling the beauty of God's Creation. Hymns like "This is My Father's World," "Earth and All Stars," and "For the Beauty of the Earth" are being sung. The emphasis of the worship services today is on celebrating the glories of what God has created on this precious, fragile planet.

When I was a pastoring a rural congregation in Pennsylvania, we had a special set of rituals for Earth Sunday. I would place a pot of soil, a watering can, and a basket of seeds on the altar and invite the children to help me bless them. Congregants would bring their garden tools and gloves, wheelbarrows, and even tractors to church. At the end of the service, we would process outside and ask for God's blessings on our labors for and with the Earth. Everyone would choose a packet of seeds from the basket and depart with the promise of spring and new life—and with the satisfaction that we would be doing our part for God's Creation.

These rituals of Creation care are right and salutary. However, there's a tragic aspect of caring for Creation that most of us are not aware of but deserves our attention.

According to *The Guardian*, Brazil saw sixty-one killings of land rights activists in 2016 and 150 since 2012. Waldomiro Costa Pereira was one of those activists. He was affiliated with the Landless Workers Movement (MST) and was killed on March 20, 2017, when half the world was celebrating the beginning of spring. Gunmen stormed the hospital in which he was recovering from a previous assassination attempt. He stood up for poor farmers and spoke out against predatory companies, a heroic act that cost him his life.

I think of Pereira and the other Earth activists when I hear these words from Revelation 14:13, "'Blessed are the dead who from now on die in the Lord.' 'Yes,' says the Spirit, 'they will rest from their labors, for their deeds follow them.'" This chapter of Revelation recounts a scene from John's apocalyptic vision where the martyrs who have followed Jesus are gathered on Mt. Zion with the Lamb, Jesus. These are the ones who have been faithful to God, who have served God's people and worship "[God] who made heaven and earth, the sea and the springs of water" (14:7). But their faithfulness and service has come at great personal cost, even losing their own lives.

Latin America has a long history of struggles over land and resources that have resulted in many people being killed. The rural poor eke out a living while those in control of the land seek to extract riches from its bounty. The murder of environmental activists is not new; it's been happening for more than thirty years. But with the growing crisis of climate change, there is increased desperation of people fighting for their communities and their very lives.

Take for instance Luiz Alberto Araújo, a Brazilian government official in the environmental office who fought tirelessly and courageously against corruption and oppression. He had broken up a deforestation operation that relied on slave labor. He reported a hydroelectric dam operator for causing the death of sixteen tons of fish. And he helped shut down a gold mine that was poisoning an indigenous tribe's food supply. But in 2016 he was shot dead in his car in front of his family.

These are the people we need to remember—those who are dying for God's Earth and for indigenous communities. This Earth Day we need to tell the truth: there is a life-and-death struggle being waged against corrupt governments, companies, and criminal gangs that are seizing land from people in order to meet the market for minerals, timber, and fossil fuels. We in developed countries may condemn these barbaric acts. But the demand for these products comes from us, particularly in the United States.

Since its earliest days, the church has honored the martyrs who die for their faith. From Stephen to Perpetua to Ignatius of Antioch, martyrs are models of courage in the face of hatred, fear, evil, oppression, and persecution. They refuse to cower to violent regimes, and they face their deaths knowing they have fought the good fight. Certain days of the church year are dedicated to their memory with prayers offered in thanksgiving for their witness.

I suggest that Earth Day be a time to venerate the Earth martyrs. They are models of courage for refusing to renounce their faith in the sacredness

Revelation 14:1–13

of Earth and indigenous communities, in the virtues of integrity and radical compassion, without which the human species will dwindle to extinction. These murdered men and women of Brazil, Columbia, Peru, the Philippines, and many other countries have, in fact, been martyred, and they need to be mourned and honored as the heroes they are. Some of them, in fact, do this work precisely because of their faith in Jesus.

Take, for instance, Dorothy Stang, an American Catholic sister who had served in Brazil. She worked on behalf of the poor and the environment by standing up to loggers and landowners. Sister Dorothy dedicated her life to defending the rainforest against deforestation and worked as an advocate for the rural poor for decades. She also tried to protect peasants from criminal gangs sent by ranchers who were after their small parcels of land. "I don't want to flee, nor do I want to abandon the battle of these farmers who live without any protection in the forest," she said. "They have the sacrosanct right to aspire to a better life on land where they can live and work with dignity while respecting the environment."

But in 2005 she was followed by two men as she walked to a community meeting about rights for the Amazon. They asked if she had any weapons, and she stated that her only weapon was her Bible. She then read a passage from the Beatitudes, "Blessed are the poor in spirit . . ." They held her at gunpoint and then shot her.[13]

"Then I saw another angel flying in midheaven, with an eternal gospel to proclaim to those who live on the earth—to every nation and tribe and language and people. He said in a loud voice, 'Fear God and give him glory, for the hour of his judgment has come'" (14:6–7). Revelation assures us that there will be judgment for those who kill the saints of God. In the meantime, we are called to "the endurance of the saints, those who keep the commandments of God and hold fast to the faith of Jesus" (14:12).

Sister Dorothy and her fellow eco-martyrs exemplify the sacrificial love of God who steadfastly proclaims that those most vulnerable—including Earth itself—are worth dying for. Their faithfulness humbles me and calls me to account. In the words of Revelation 14:4–5 "They have been redeemed from humankind as first fruits for God and the Lamb, and in their mouth no lie was found; they are blameless."

So this Earth Day, I'm standing in solidarity with the Earth martyrs and praying that I may have such dedication and courage. I'm trusting in the mercy of a Creator who declared this planet good, not for the sake of

---

13. Sisters of Notre Dame de Namur, "Expanded Story of Sister Dorothy Stang."

commodification but simply because it exists. That existence is threatened more each day, so I can no longer take it for granted.

On Earth Day this year let's pick up more than seed packets. Let's take up the cross. And let's remember that eco-crucifixion is eventually followed by eco-resurrection. Because even as we are remembering the Earth martyrs, we need to tell the stories of new life in places where they are, in fact, recovering from environmental devastation and renewing their relationship with God's Creation. Places like El Salvador where, with the support of the Catholic Church, they recently banned all metal mining in favor of protecting its fragile water systems. Places like Mexico, which has moved to designate 160 million acres of land for environmental conservation. And across the globe, young people following the lead of teen activist Greta Thunberg are rising up for action on the climate crisis.

John's vision in Revelation puts the systems of domination on notice: the crucifixions they perpetrate will not be the final word, nor will their oppressive reign endure without resistance. The Lamb, the resurrected one, will open our eyes to Creation "liberated from its bondage to decay and brought into the freedom and glory of the children of God" (Rom 8:21). So when we sing our hymns celebrating God's Creation today, remember that they are more than just pretty anthems. They are songs of resistance sung with that great gathering on Mt. Zion.

"I heard a voice from heaven like the sound of many waters and like the sound of loud thunder; the voice I heard was like the sound of harpists playing on their harps, and they sing a new song before the throne" (Rev 14:2–3). This is the song of faith, of endurance, of divine love for the martyrs and for the Earth. This is our song and their song—the music of God and of the Lamb. Thanks be to God.

Chapter 11

Revelation 21:1-6
(Year C—Easter—Fifth Sunday of Easter)

¹Then I saw a new heaven and a new earth; for the first heaven and the first earth had passed away, and the sea was no more. ²And I saw the holy city, the new Jerusalem, coming down out of heaven from God, prepared as a bride adorned for her husband. ³And I heard a loud voice from the throne saying, "See, the home of God is among mortals. He will dwell with them as their God; they will be his peoples, and God himself will be with them; ⁴he will wipe every tear from their eyes. Death will be no more; mourning and crying and pain will be no more, for the first things have passed away." ⁵And the one who was seated on the throne said, "See, I am making all things new." Also he said, "Write this, for these words are trustworthy and true." ⁶Then he said to me, "It is done! I am the Alpha and the Omega, the beginning and the end. To the thirsty I will give water as a gift from the spring of the water of life.

AN EXEGESIS OF REVELATION 21:1-6

Jerry L. Sumney

This text follows the final judgment scene in chapters 17—18. There Rome is defeated and condemned. Then Satan and all who oppose God's purposes are judged and condemned. The only people left are those whose names are in the Book of Life (20:15). This judgment is as necessary as the salvation of the faithful is necessary. It is a demonstration of God's justice, a necessary divine attribute. The judgment of the wicked who have persecuted God's people and the salvation of the faithful are two aspects of the same eschatological act. Both are necessary for God to express the fullness of God's justice, mercy, and love. Both are demonstrations that God is indeed sovereign, even when it seems that evil has more power in the present.

As soon as John finishes describing the judgment of the wicked, he says, "And I saw a new heaven and new earth" (21:1). It is a new vision, but intimately related to the previous one. John seems to draw the image of a new heaven and earth from Isaiah 65:17, a text that describes the final glorious restoration of Jerusalem and the people of God. There, the former things are remembered no more; here in Revelation the former things are no more. In 20:11 the heaven and earth fled from before God's judgment; now that void is filled with the new heaven and earth. They are made new, but the sea has been done away with. The sea was a symbol of chaos and rebellion against God; such powers no longer threaten God's people, or even exist. In John's first vision of heaven, the sea had been tamed; it was a sea of glass (4:6). God had taken control of it so that it could not threaten, but it still existed. In the final state of things, it is gone. Nothing will threaten the security of God's people.

The creation of the new heaven and earth does not suggest a complete discontinuity with the previous heaven and earth, however. In fact, the New Jerusalem, the place of the presence of God, is coming down to the world. So, there is some continuity. As Eugene Boring notes, "God does not make 'all new things,' but 'all things new.'"[1] This suggests that God is concerned about the creation, as the new is constructed out of the old. If God's plan involves the reclamation of God's good creation (see also Rom 8:19–23), then believers, as those who seek God's will, should be involved in this task. As we will see, the description of this wonderful salvation is an exhortation to faithfulness in doing God's will.

Further, God is not abandoning the original creation; the New Jerusalem is coming down to where the people are. This coming down of the New Jerusalem also means that the saved are not taken up from this world. While other imagery in the New Testament has imagery of going up, here God brings the salvation to the people and the creation.

---

1. Boring cited by Blount, *Revelation*, 376.

Throughout this description of the New Jerusalem, John draws on imagery from Isaiah 60—65 with its description of the glorification of Jerusalem that is coming when God acts to give Israel its place in the world as God's people. John describes this new Jerusalem as a holy city. When the Bible uses the language of holiness for God, it refers to both God's distinctiveness (because no one is like God) and to God's moral character. Both of these ideas seem to be present in this description of Jerusalem. After all, since it is God's place of residence, it must reflect the character of God. It also means that those who live in it must be holy, as 21:7–8 makes explicit.

John again (as in 18:23, 21:9, 22:17) uses the image of a bride for the church because he sees the relationship between God and the church as so close that this metaphor is appropriate. Even as John has been exhorting his readers to faithfulness, he says here that God has prepared the New Jerusalem so that it is dressed like a bride on her wedding day. The readers must remain faithful, but God is enabling that faithfulness. John is mixing his metaphors here as the New Jerusalem is both the place and the people who live in it. But he is seeking effect, not consistency in metaphors. He wants readers to see this sight as one of indescribable beauty.

In v. 3, an unidentified voice from God's throne says God's "tent" (*skēnos*) will be among the people, and the term he uses for "living" among them is the verb form of "tent" (*skēnoō*). This is the terminology that the Septuagint (the Greek translation of the Hebrew Bible) used for the tabernacle the Israelites had in their wilderness wandering. (It is also the language the Gospel of John uses to describe the incarnation in 1:14.) Some interpreters see John's use of this terminology as an allusion that relates this final eschatological act to the exodus and to God's dwelling with the people in the wilderness. This makes the exodus a pattern to which this final act conforms. Whether that is the case or not, the image intends to convey the closest proximity possible. God will live directly with the people. They will not be kept back by temple walls because they live in God's tent/tabernacle. They are fully God's people and fully in God's presence. In that presence, God fully claims them as God's own.

This voice also proclaims that God's new creation will be a place where there is no more sorrow because all the reasons for it will be gone. There will be no pain and no death. The voice declares that suffering, sorrow, and grief were part of the "first things" that are now gone. The new creation is a place of life and joy.

Then John wants his readers to be absolutely certain that this is the future that God guarantees the faithful. He does this by having God, Godself, make the promise. This is only the second time in the book that God speaks. Here God tells John to write this assurance: "these words are faithful and true." Then he tells John that these things are done. The end has come; God has now fulfilled God's promises. This future is so sure that God declares it a completed task in this vision.

In both places where God speaks in Revelation (1:8; 21:5–8), God proclaims Godself the Alpha and Omega. These are, of course, the first and last letters of the Greek alphabet. This designation identifies God as the origin of all things and God as the one who consummates all things. Everything of all time is subject to God. This proclamation asserts the sovereignty of God over all things, assuring the readers that the promise of salvation is guaranteed.

The aspect of the future John emphasizes here is that God gives all who come water from the spring of water that gives life. "Living water" is the expression in Greek for what we call "running water." But it is clear here that it means water that gives eternal life, as it did in Jesus' conversation with the Samaritan woman in John 4:10–15. In the face of persecution that might lead to death, then, God promises a new and fuller life in God's presence for those who are faithful.

Our reading stops in the middle of a paragraph. The next two verses say that those who are faithful will receive this blessed new life with God, but those who capitulate in the persecution or live sinful lives will be turned away. As we have noted before, the point of talking about the salvation to come is not to divert our attention from life in the present. Rather, the point is to encourage believers to be faithful to God's will in this world. As John assumes that such faithfulness will bring disadvantage in the present, he reminds his readers that accepting the disadvantage and suffering will be more than worth it.

Revelation 21:1–6

IDEAS FOR PREACHING ON REVELATION 21:1-6

Leah D. Schade

Casting a vision of hope in the midst of despair

When preaching about apocalyptic texts, preachers will need to guide their congregations through a certain amount of disorientation and ambiguity found in passages like Revelation 21. Such guidance entails several challenging tasks. They must be honest about the difficulties we face in this world while not leaving listeners bereft of hope or paralyzed with fear. They must also avoid neatly wrapped sermonic packages of empty optimism or end-time fantasies that distract us from the work of Christ in the here and now. Sumney notes that John's purpose in Revelation is not to divert our attention away from the present world. Rather, we are to discern God's will and act upon it, even when such action brings hardship. The preacher can reinforce John's message by drawing attention to our calling to care for those in need, even when doing so entails a cost.

Guiding a congregation through apocalyptic texts also means emphasizing the gospel. Ronald J. Allen urges preachers not to neglect speaking concretely about God's promises even while critiquing contemporary empires. "Many people are more motivated for long-term commitment by promise and possibility than by fear, threat, and anger. While the critique is important, preaching is often especially empowering when it aims towards a vision of the positively possible and toward helping people imagine how to get from there to here."[2] Key to this vision-casting is not looking to the skies to see souls raptured up to heaven, but to notice how God's holy city is coming *down* to Earth. The sermon can share stories and illustrations showing what patience and faithfulness look like while awaiting the new Jerusalem.

Inverting Rapture theology

Both Allen and Sumney highlight the fact that Revelation 21 counters the premillennialist theory of a "Rapture" where believers are whisked up to

---

2. Allen, *I Will Tell You the Mystery*, 198.

the clouds and the sinners and non-Christians are left behind in a sort of earthly purgatory. Sumney clarifies that "God is not abandoning the original creation, [instead] the New Jerusalem is coming down to where the people are. This coming down of the New Jerusalem also means that the saved are not taken up from this world. While other imagery in the New Testament has imagery of going up, here God brings the salvation to the people and the creation." Allen notes how this downward movement "embodies grace itself: God takes the initiative to bring the holy city *down* from heaven."[3]

Thus, hope for the new creation is neither spiritualized wishful thinking nor an escape from the reality of our crucified world. There is both transcendence and immanence in Christ's return and the new creation. They are not mutually exclusive, but instead inform each other in a dialectic exchange in which one points to the other and back again. The challenge for preachers, says Allen, is to "help the congregation look for signs of [the holy city's] appearance."[4] One way to do this is to focus on the fact that "John's Jerusalem needs no temple because the whole of it is the dwelling place of God." What are the ramifications for Christians in seeing Earth itself as God's temple? How might Creation be a site of sacredness as God's dwelling place? The sermon can help listeners notice the ways in which even now we are living in the very presence of God—even if the site of sacredness has been defiled and needs our attention in cleaning it up.

Another way to point to signs of the new creation is by highlighting work that has already been done to preserve and protect the temple of Earth, especially the *hydor zoē*, the water of life that gurgles up in verse 6. What local waterways have been cleaned of pollution and trash? How are people making strides to clean up the garbage patches in the oceans? Perhaps your congregation can contribute to efforts for creating potable water sources in drought-prone places. In any of these stories about caring for the precious gift of water, the preacher can connect these efforts both to the biblical text and to the liturgical image of baptism's cleansing, renewing waters. The sermon should emphasize that the church's work in Creation care is consistent with what God wants for the world now and what God will bring about for all Creation in the fulfillment of time.

---

3. Allen, *I Will Tell You the Mystery*, 200.
4. Allen, *I Will Tell You the Mystery*, 200.

Revelation 21:1–6

Challenges of preaching "a new heaven and a new earth"

The book of Revelation contains prophetic visions of what God is doing to bring about a world that is radically different from the broken, sinful, poisoned, dying one in which we now live. In chapter 21, the city of Jerusalem is both the symbol and focal point of the new age in which pain, sorrow, and devastation are but a distant memory. God's transformation of what we once knew will lead to a relationship of reconciliation between humanity, God, and all of Creation. The text is hopeful, confident, and enthusiastic about the future in light of God's promises.

The difficulty, however, is that throughout Christian history, Revelation has been interpreted by many in a way that renders the created world inadequate and doomed to be replaced by the new creation. H. Paul Santmire notes that in the eschatology of many Christian thinkers, nature is either viewed as evil and inferior and needing to be conquered, or left behind at the end of the age, or as merely a stage and backdrop for the salvation drama between God and humanity.[5] Santmire traces the historical background of how current theologies of nature are correspondingly shaped by how we view "the end" of nature. For example, one can see the effects of early polemics against the "heresy" of heathen Earth-worshipers recapitulated as an Earth-be-damned attitude inherent in millennialism that focuses solely on the salvation of born-again Christians.

At the same time, overconfidence in a patriarchal sky-god sending down the new creation to erase our sins, ecological and otherwise, can lead to us to shirk our responsibilities for caring for the Creation in the present time. "A new heaven and earth" may sound to some like an advertisement about a product that is "new and improved" in our consumerist economy. This is the kind of thinking that contributes to a maddening cycle of frantic accumulation and reckless disposal that alternatingly strips and chokes our planet and vulnerable communities with overconsumption and pollution.

Sumney points out, in contrast, that "the creation of the new heaven and earth does not suggest a complete discontinuity with the previous heaven and earth. In fact, the New Jerusalem, the place of the presence of God, is coming down to the world. So, there is some continuity." With this in mind, the preacher can invite the congregation to consider ways they can be involved in the task of reclaiming and renewing God's good Creation. How that materializes in the sermon will depend on the context

---

5. Santmire, *The Travail of Nature*.

of the church and the vision discerned through conversations with church members about what this renewal of Creation might look like in their time and place.

Revelation 21:1–6

"THIS WORLD IT IS MY HOME"

A Sermon on Revelation 21:1–6

Leah D. Schade

(I preached this sermon at R. B. Winter State Park near Mifflinburg, Pennsylvania, for our church's annual camping retreat in 2015. The texts for the day were Revelation 21:1–7 and John 1:1–4, 14–18. With our own tents in the background, the biblical image of God's tent, skēnos, *took on a different perspective as we thought about Jesus "camping" among us.)*

We once had a famous singing group at our church that gifted us with wonderful hymns and songs of praise. At one point in the program they did a medley of what I call "old chestnuts," the songs of faith that go back generations and have a soft spot in people's hearts and memories. Songs like "In the Garden" and "This Little Light of Mine."

But there was one snippet of a song that gave me pause. The song is called "This World is Not My Home," and it includes these lyrics:

> This world is not my home, I'm just a-passin' through.
> My treasures are laid up somewhere beyond the blue.
> The angels beckon me from heaven's open door.
> And I can't feel at home in this world anymore.[6]

On the one hand, I can appreciate the sentiment of someone drawing near to the end of a difficult life and desiring to be with the Lord and see their loved ones who dwell in heaven. But the idea that this world—which we know God created out of God's divine love—is not our home, and that we're just passing through, is problematic. Because if this world is not my home, then I really don't have a reason to care about it.

In fact, some people treat this Earth as nothing but a hotel room on our soul's journey to heaven. We're just here on a temporary stay in a place not worth caring about. When people go into a hotel, they expect that someone is going to clean up their mess, straighten up the clutter, scrub off the soap

---

6. "This World is Not My Home" is sometimes attributed to Albert Edward Brumley (1905–1977). However, research indicates that the first appearance of the song seems to have been in the 1919 *Joyful Meeting in Glory* No. 1, edited by Bertha Davis and published by C. Miller of Mt. Sterling, KY. Therefore, the song is in the public domain.

scum on the shower walls, and empty the trash. We have no attachment to that room. We've got no "skin in the game," so to speak. And it makes no difference to us who will stay in it after we leave. This room is not my home.

Of course, if I had that attitude in my own home, what would happen? I would end up living in a filthy, junked-up mess.

Perhaps that partly explains the state of the Earth in which we find ourselves. A theology that teaches us that the world is not our home leaves no room for caring about God's Creation. Such an attitude means that we have no attachment to this place. It divorces our thoughts and feelings from how we treat the Earth and what we will leave for those who will live here after we're gone.

It's no wonder, then, that we produce trash that is overflowing the landfills, choking wildlife, and creating entire islands in the ocean of floating plastic. We mine and dig and extract the fossil fuels for our energy needs and end up poisoning our waterways, fouling our air, and blanketing Earth with carbon dioxide that is disrupting our planet's climate cycles.

We live as if this world is not our home, that we are just a'passin' through. That our treasure is not in these green mountains or pristine waterways, but "laid up somewhere beyond the blue." It's like we're having a huge party in our hotel room with seven billion of our friends, and we're just trashing the place, expecting the maids to clean it up and the management to foot the bill.

But of course, there are no magical maids. There are just lots and lots of people left wallowing in heaps of trash, dying from cancers caused by environmental toxins, and fleeing their island homes because the waters are literally swallowing their coastlines. What we forget is that "the management" is going to hold us accountable. We live as if there's a Big Daddy in the sky who will take us up to heaven with him and let this world literally go to hell. This kind of theology leads to corporate decisions, government policies, and individual choices that reinforce the belief that this world is not my home. But it's not what the writers of Scripture intended.

In fact, when we read the words from the Gospel of John, we get a very different impression about who God is, what's important to God, and how God feels about this Earth:

> In the beginning was the Word, and the Word was with God, and the Word was God. He was in the beginning with God. All things came into being through him, and without him not one thing came into being. What has come into being in him was life, and

the life was the light of all people. The light shines in the darkness, and the darkness did not overcome it . . .And the Word became flesh and lived among us (John 1:1–5, 14).

Did you hear that? The Word became flesh. This means God actually *does* have skin in the game. Jesus was a real, living person who dwelled on this Earth, drank this water, walked on this soil. Jesus lived among us. The Greek word here is *skēnoō*. In English we translate it as "dwell," but the word literally means "to put up a tent." It's the same word used in Revelation 21:3: "See, the home of God is among mortals. He will *dwell* with them as their God; they will be his peoples, and God himself will be with them."

Think about that for a minute. Jesus, as God's Word made flesh, pitched a tent among us! He shared meals around campfires and cooked fish on the beach for his friends. He took long walks with them and had meaningful conversations. He played with children. And Jesus often encouraged his disciples to take time away from their work of ministry to simply enjoy the world God had made, just as we are doing on this retreat.

I've been thinking a lot about tenting this weekend. Going camping is no easy task. There's a lot involved with packing everything up, traveling to the site, setting up the tent, planning and cooking the meals, and keeping an eye out for critters both annoying and dangerous. But there's also something about setting up camp and spending time in the woods with people who are important to you that is deeply meaningful. The shared meals around the campfire. The long walks exploring God's Creation along creeks and hiking trails. The time away from work and technology that opens up space for breathing, long conversations, and playfulness. This is what I imagine when I hear John's description of "a new heaven and a new earth" in Revelation. God is making all things new in us and through us as we care for the very Earth with which God has entrusted us.

So if Jesus, the Word made flesh, tented with us, doesn't that mean that he considered this Earth his home? And if this is God's home, do we dare trash it like a hotel room?

Revelation shares a vision of the world not as a place to be trashed and thrown away, but as God's very temple and throne. Here at R. B. Winter State Park, in this place in nature that is protected and preserved for us and future generations, we catch a glimpse of what God has in mind for us. As we splash in clean, clear water in the lake fed by the cold mountain stream, we can imagine God baptizing the Earth in a continual flow of sacred water. This is what God wants for us—"a gift from the spring of the water of life."

Isn't this the kind of Earth we want? Isn't this the kind of community we want? Where no one will go hungry because there is equitable sharing of food and resources. Where there will be no more thirst because waters run clean and pure, droughts are but a memory, and pollution is cleaned up. Where the sun's heat will not be trapped within the atmosphere by greenhouse gases. Where darkness is no longer feared. Where worshiping the Lamb, the vulnerable one, means caring for the most vulnerable lambs among us—unborn children, infants, children, and pregnant mothers. Where our decisions about what we buy and what we drive and how we grow our food will be governed by the needs of "the least of these." This is the kind of world John envisioned.

Because as the Gospel of John reminds us, God so loved *the world* (John 3:16). This world. This soil. This tree. That bird. This human. They all say: the world, it *is* my home.

God, indeed, is with us, and dwells among us. Jesus, the Word made flesh, beckons us to sing different words to the song:

> This world it *is* our home. We're not just passin' through.
> Our treasures are found here *and* beyond the blue.
> The Spirit beckons us from Earth's open door.
> And we can finally feel at home on Earth once more.

Chapter 12

Revelation 21:10, 22—22:5

(Year C—Easter—Sixth Sunday of Easter)

¹⁰*And in the spirit he carried me away to a great, high mountain and showed me the holy city Jerusalem coming down out of heaven from God . . .* ²²*I saw no temple in the city, for its temple is the Lord God the Almighty and the Lamb.* ²³*And the city has no need of sun or moon to shine on it, for the glory of God is its light, and its lamp is the Lamb.* ²⁴*The nations will walk by its light, and the kings of the earth will bring their glory into it.* ²⁵*Its gates will never be shut by day—and there will be no night there.* ²⁶*People will bring into it the glory and the honor of the nations.* ²⁷*But nothing unclean will enter it, nor anyone who practices abomination or falsehood, but only those who are written in the Lamb's book of life.*
²²:¹*Then the angel showed me the river of the water of life, bright as crystal, flowing from the throne of God and of the Lamb* ²*through the middle of the street of the city. On either side of the river is the tree of life with its twelve kinds of fruit, producing its fruit each month; and the leaves of the tree are for the healing of the nations.* ³*Nothing accursed will be found there any more. But the throne of God and of the Lamb will be in it, and his servants will worship him;* ⁴*they will see his face, and his name will be on their foreheads.* ⁵*And there will be no more night; they need no light of lamp or sun, for the Lord God will be their light, and they will reign forever and ever.*

Apocalypse When?
An Exegesis of Revelation 21:10, 22—22:5

Jerry L. Sumney

In the previous chapter on Revelation 14, we talked about the occasion and purposes of Revelation. We do not need to repeat that here. We should remember that Revelation is written to a church that is being persecuted. John helps them interpret that persecution and assures them that in the final state of all things, God will be victorious over evil. John also exhorts them to remain faithful by assuring them that the faithful will live in that blessed state with God.

As Revelation 21:1–6 introduced the final and climactic vision of the book, this reading concludes it. We saw above that John sees the new Jerusalem when he sees the new heaven and earth. In 21:9–10 he reintroduces the new Jerusalem to contrast it with the introduction to his vision of the condemnation of Babylon in 17:1–3. In both, one of the angels with the bowls full of God's wrath call John and "show" him the scene. In chapter 17 the angel takes John to the desert, the place of temptation and rebellion against God. In 21:9–10 the angel takes John to a high mountain, the place of meeting God's presence and of revelation from God. The condemnation and destruction of Babylon (Rome) follows the trip to the desert, while the description of the blessed city follows the trip to the mountain. With these parallels in language and action, John ties together the condemnation of the wicked and the salvation of the faithful. They are both necessary parts of the single final act that makes all things what God intends.

Between that reintroduction of the new Jerusalem and the resumption of our reading, John describes the walls and gates of the new city. He draws on Ezekiel's vision of the new temple (Ezek 40–44) as he tells of the enormous size and beauty of the new city. Verse 22 opens John's portrayal of an important and surprising aspect of the city. He says there is no temple in this city. John's Jerusalem needs no temple because the whole of it is the dwelling place of God. The whole place *is* a temple. When Ezekiel envisioned God coming to live among God's people, he said that there would only be a wall between God and the people because they would build their houses right beside the temple (43:8). He sees that as an amazing display of God's intimate presence among God's people. John goes far beyond that; he removes all barriers between God and God's people. There is no wall that separates God's presence and glory from the people, no intermediaries between them. This life lived in the very presence of God is an amazing promise.

Further, the glory of God and the Lamb shine so brightly that there is no need for the sun and moon. It is common to describe God's glory, God's reputation and honor, as something that shines brightly. This image of God's intimate presence draws on Isaiah 60:19, where Isaiah sees the day coming when the sun and moon will no longer be needed because the light of God's glory will be all the light the people of God need.

It is something of a surprise when John sees the nations basking in the divine light and bringing their treasures into the holy city. In the judgment scene of chapters 17–18, it seemed that they were destroyed. Perhaps they turn to God here because Satan and his instrument Rome have been defeated and dispatched. They are no longer there to deceive the nations, so the nations now honor God as they should. Instead of bringing gifts to Rome to prove their loyalty, the kings of the nations now bring those gifts to God. This is another sign that God is sovereign. All the governments recognize God's power and status as ruler of the cosmos. Some interpreters see here a hint that John has a vision of something close to universal salvation. After all, if the rebellious kings and governments who followed Rome are now enjoying the end-time blessings, then God must save all people. But as if to dissuade readers from the idea that how one lives on earth does not determine one's end-time fate, the very next verse says that sinners will not be permitted in the holy city (21:27). The point of having the kings submit to God seems to point more to an emphasis on God's sovereignty and the extent to which it will be exercised and recognized.

At 22:1 John takes up new imagery to try to express how magnificent and grace-filled this existence with God will be. He draws on the Genesis description of Eden. It is not uncommon in apocalyptic literature for the blessed end-time to be a return to the pure state of Eden. John takes elements of that kind of description and magnifies them. In Genesis a river flows out of Eden that supplies water to the world (2:10–14), but in Revelation a river flows out of the throne of God and the Lamb and down the middle of the main street of the city. It is a river whose waters give life (22:1) and the river that nourishes the Tree of Life. John's imagery again outstrips logic and physical possibility as he describes the Tree of Life. He constantly talks about the singular Tree of Life, but there are twelve of this one tree and they grow on both sides of the street. The intent of the singular is to identify it with the Tree of Life in Eden (3:21–24) and then to best that tree by having it twelve times. More than this, it has a new flavor every month! John wants life in the new Jerusalem to be as full and satisfying as his readers can imagine.

This tree does even more; its leaves heal the nations. This is the second time the nations have been part of this vision of the blessed existence of the faithful. The nations as communities and as political and social structures seem to need special attention. John recognizes that the governing political and economic systems of his day are unjust and thus in need of healing. We should recognize the same things about our political and economic systems that privilege the wealthy and the advantaged. Our economic systems offer lower interest rates to the wealthy and we take advantage of people working in sweatshops around the world so we can have cheap clothes and phones. John would point out that our systems are ruled by the powers of evil, just as he saw Rome ruling by the powers of evil. All such systems in the world continue to be unjust and in need of the healing John here envisions. John promises that the final state of things will include an existence governed by the justice and mercy of God.

But John may also have in mind another aspect of this salvation, its corporate nature. He is not describing this city from the perspective of the salvation of just the individual. Nations, as communities and societies, are being healed. Some interpreters suggest that this is the significance of John's use of a city to describe life with God. An urban description requires the salvation to be communal as well as individual.[1] The end-time life is not just "me and God" in a quietistic daze; it is communal life in active fellowship with those who together love and praise God.

There is perhaps one other reference to the Eden story. In v. 3 John says that a curse is no longer there. Situated between the description of the Tree of Life and the promise of being in God's presence, this may be a reference to the curse in Genesis 3:14–19. God puts Adam and Eve out of God's presence and the Garden and away from the Tree of Life. Then comes the curse that describes the unjust social and familial structures of the world and the difficulties of providing for one's living. John may have that curse in mind here. If so, this is another way that he sees this end-time reversing the effects of the Fall and returning existence to the state God intended. At the least, the absence of any curse means that evil can no longer harm God's people.

---

1. Blount, *Revelation*, 377–78.

Revelation 21:10, 22—22:5

In place of the curse, the throne of God and the Lamb are present. John has been drawing the identity of God and the Lamb closer to each other as the book has progressed. At the beginning the Lamb can enter the throne area (5:6–8) and then is associated with the throne, but not seated on it (7:9–17). Worship is given the Lamb that is appropriate only for God from its first appearance (5:9–14) and on through the book. In our passage, God and the Lamb are the temple (21:22) that alleviates the need for a visible temple. Then, the divine glory that makes the sun and moon unnecessary also comes from God and the Lamb. John draws Christ into the divinity of God ever more closely as both are the temple and both radiate the divine glory that lights the blessed existence of the faithful. Finally, in 22:1 and 3, the throne in heaven is the throne of God and the Lamb. This brings their identity as close as it can be. John has no theory of the Trinity, but he sees Christ as one associated with the divine in a way that makes it appropriate to worship him and no other being except God and that allows God's throne to be Christ's as well.

John begins the conclusion of his depiction of the new Jerusalem with another surprise: the servants of God who now worship God in the city see God's face directly. Throughout most of Scripture, humans are not able to look at God's face and live. Not even Moses was allowed to see God's face (Exod 33:20–23). The descriptions of the presence of God in Revelation before this have been more abstract, speaking of the brightness of jewels, for example (4:3). But the final state of existence for the faithful will bring them so intimately into the presence of God that they will see God's face directly. This intimacy is mirrored in God's claiming of them as God's own by having God's name written on their foreheads.

John returns to the notion that the glory of God obviates the need for any other source of light, but this time adds that night never comes to the holy city. The glory of God shines there continuously. This image says that the people in the city will be completely secure. There will be no darkness that might give cover to danger. In the description of the walls and the gates of the city, John has already said that those gates never close because there is no need. The forces of evil have been permanently dispatched and the presence of God keeps all the city safe (21:11–21). This is an important message for churches that are enduring persecution. Their lives in the present are never wholly safe. They must constantly be on their guard, knowing that the ruling powers wish them harm. John assures these churches that God will give them a completely secure life.

John ends the portrayal of the blessed life with God by saying that the faithful will "reign forever and ever" (22:5). They seem to share in God's rule of the world. Perhaps this is one more way for John to assure the readers of the complete reversal of positions that awaits them if they remain faithful. Instead of being abused by those who reign, they will be the ones reigning. Further, John has said repeatedly that the rule of Satan and of Rome are temporary. The reign of the faithful will be permanent because God is the one who guarantees it.

This amazing depiction of life with God at the End is designed to encourage faithfulness. Even as John has Jesus speak some closing words, Jesus says that each will get what their works indicate they should receive (22:12). This is not a kind of legalism, but it again reinforces that the purpose of this portrayal of post-mortem bliss is to encourage faithfulness to God's will in the present. For the first readers, that meant holding on to their faith in the face of persecution. Only in this way could they shape a small part of the world into a place that reflects the will of God for the whole world. In the present, such texts call the church to work to make the world a place that reflects God's will, a place that reflects God's justice, love, and mercy.

Revelation 21:10, 22—22:5

IDEAS FOR PREACHING

Leah D. Schade

A river runs through it

The prominence of the river flowing from the throne of God and the Lamb in Revelation 22 offers opportunities for the preacher to address any number of issues around water. Everyone must have clean water for drinking, bathing, and irrigating crops, and every community has challenges in providing potable water for its citizens. The preacher can invite listeners to consider their local watershed or closest body of water to the church. And then ask: what is the biggest source of water pollution in our area? What is the role of the church in protecting the waters of Creation in which we baptize?

The sermon could utilize a four-page form wherein the preacher points to Revelation 8 and the ways in which water has been poisoned and sea creatures are dying today, but then contrasts that with Revelation 22 and the vision of the crystal-clear waters flowing from God's throne. What are ways in which people are living into this vision now? Sharing stories of faith communities working to create sources of clean water, or protesting the pollution of water, or cleaning up local streams or rivers and even the ocean itself, can help people understand God's intention for this Earth and all communities. As Ronald J. Allen notes, "The river of life flows through the middle of the city so the water is available to all. Water is not distributed according to one's place in the social pyramid."[2]

Allen also notes that while John does not indicate that the river is intended as a symbol for baptism, the imagery provides a theologically compelling framework for this sacrament. The preacher could encourage fellow congregants to join with a local group committed to cleaning up the waterways in their area. This can be framed as a spiritual practice of stewarding the waters and living out an eschatological faith in God's restorative work for Creation.

---

2. Allen, *I Will Tell You the Mystery*, 214.

Trees of Life in abundance

Sumney notes that the abundant number of the Trees of Life "is to identify it with the Tree of Life in Eden (3:21–24) and then to best that tree by having it twelve times. More than this, it has a new flavor every month! John wants life in the new Jerusalem to be as full and satisfying as his readers can imagine." The preacher can point out that God, in fact, has already provided more than enough trees which provide the very air we breathe. Trees are the lungs of our planet, exhaling oxygen even as we breathe out the carbon dioxide they need.

As Matthew Sleeth observes in his book *Reforesting Faith*, if you look at the cast of the human respiratory tree, you'll see that it is indistinguishable from the shape of a bare oak tree. "I've come to understand that one of the most important reasons God chose trees is that at every stage of their lives, trees give. Yet some thirty-six football fields worth of forest are cut down worldwide every minute. Less than half are replanted."[3]

Trees *are* life—they exist virtually every place that humans live on this planet. When trees are plentiful and healthy, people are healthy. A sermon focusing on the Tree of Life in Revelation 22 can urge listeners to act in a way that demonstrates respect both for God's Word and for God's trees. The sacred exchange is something that God, future generations, and every living thing on Earth can celebrate together.

Leaves for healing

The preacher can also use this image of the trees healing the nations to highlight that nearly every religion uses the image of the tree to convey the sacred linkage between sky and earth, the realm of the divine and the realm of humanity. As I note in *For the Beauty of the Earth: A Lenten Devotional*:

> The tree embodies the mysterious interchange of birth, growth, death, and new life; of soil, water, air, and sunlight; of reaching into the depths while also rising toward the heights. As we witness the ongoing and accelerating degradation of the planetary life-systems that support trees . . . these great woody plants suggest what we need to do in this perilous time. *Homo religiosus* must reach deep into our soil of scriptural and spiritual wisdom in order to draw up the life-giving water and nutrients that can sustain the

---

3. Sleeth, *Reforesting Faith*, 136–37.

trunk, branches, and leaves of the whole "family tree" that makes its home on Earth.[4]

Revelation 22 is a beautiful vision of the river, trees, and God's faithful community living as God intended. In addition, such a sermon can bring together both faith and science by explaining what research has revealed about the healing nature of trees. Trees release a chemical call phytoncides to keep themselves healthy, and when we breathe them into our bodies, they trigger the production of special leukocytes that strengthen the body's immune system. This means that a regular practice of walking among trees is truly healing. In fact, the Japanese have a term for this "forest therapy" called *shinrin yoku*, or "forest bathing." Our health is dependent on the health of trees and the ecosystems that support them. The preacher can suggest that Revelation's imagery supports a multi-faith ecological effort to plant, tend, protect, and preserve trees, forests, and the land and water they—and we—need to survive.

The healing of nations

A preacher wanting to focus on the healing of the nations will need to explain the ways in which the nations—the political, social, and economic systems—are ill. Allen states that "the sickness of the nations (so to speak) is idolatry. The symptoms: they worship the beast and the dragon (false gods), collude with these enemies of God, and hence, deserve punishment. The medicine is the worldview of the book of Revelation. God offers the nations the opportunity for healing (being part of the new Jerusalem) through repentance and living towards mutually supportive community."[5] The preacher can proclaim that leaves of healing are intended for all the ways in which the peoples of the world suffer from racism, sexism, ableism, poverty, misogyny, and ecological injustice.

Because salvation is meant for more than just the individual, Sumney reminds us, the preacher will need to exercise a prophetic voice regarding the communal aspect of Revelation 22: "The end-time life is not just 'me and God' in a quietistic daze; it is communal life in active fellowship with those who together love and praise God." Such divine fellowship stands in contrast to the world as it has been structured by the power of Rome

---

4. Schade, *For the Beauty of the Earth*, 25.
5. Allen, *I Will Tell You the Mystery*, 215.

and every dominating nation that has followed. Walter Brueggemann notes that "as long as the economy is monopolized by an imperial superpower [whether Rome or the United States], the nations cannot enjoy a healthy existence."[6] One task of this sermon, then, will be to expose the ways in which we accept hegemony as normative and what the costs are of refusing to speak out or otherwise resist these systemic powers. "The hope that propels faith is not escapism from socioeconomic, political reality," says Brueggemann. "It is rather a resolve that all such social reality should be ordered by the rule of Christ according to the neighbor law of love."[7]

Could the church be seen as a form of the Tree of Life? As Sumney puts it, the faithful community is called to shape a small part of the world into a place that reflects the will of God." Tying the eschatological to the ecclesial, the preacher could make the case that the church can be an intentional environment for God's healing, justice, and fullness of life to flourish. The sermon can open a rhetorical space for this by pointing to examples of God's holy community revealing itself, even if through a mirror dimly. Reinforcing the values of equity, inclusivity, nonviolence, forgiveness, and ethical justice are goals for such a sermon.

---

6. Brueggemann, *Money and Possessions*, 278.

7. Brueggemann, *Money and Possessions*, 278.

Revelation 21:10, 22—22:5

"SHALL WE GATHER AT THE RIVER"

A Sermon on Revelation 21:10, 22—22:5

Leah D. Schade

(This sermon was preached as the culmination of a series entitled "Rivers in the Bible" at Reformation Lutheran Church in Media, Pennsylvania, in 2004. I used a forty-foot stretch of fabric with a water pattern placed at a different location in the sanctuary each week to highlight the significance of water in the biblical story and in our liturgical setting. On this last Sunday, the cloth was hung from the cross and draped over the altar, giving the visual impression of a river flowing from the "throne" and out into the congregation. While the sermon contains a prophetic call for the church to be the "tree of life," it ends in with a call and response in celebration leading into the well-known hymn, "Shall We Gather at the River?" by Robert Lowry, written in 1864.)

I love a surprise ending! Have you ever watched a movie by director M. Night Shyamalan? Ever seen *The Sixth Sense*? *Signs*? *The Village*? Every one of those movies ends with a twist. Suspense is built up throughout the movie because there's a struggle going on, and you're not sure how it's going to end. But then there is that moment when the truth is revealed, and you're left breathless, realizing what was there all along, but you never noticed it until the end.

Did you know that the Bible has a surprise ending? It's here in the last chapter of the last book of Revelation. Revelation was written by a man named John living on the island of Patmos in the Mediterranean Sea sometime between the years 60 and 100 CE. Much has been written about the bizarre symbolism in this apocalyptic book, particularly by Christians seeking hidden codes about the end times. But scholars agree that John of Patmos was writing in a particular time in history about a particular situation that the early Christians faced—the domination of the Roman Empire and the persecution of Christians.

Revelation does have relevance for our modern world, but it's not to be used as a cryptic code for predicting the future. Instead, it helps us critique current social structures and the domination system that oppresses and persecutes so many people. Revelation portrays this as a life-and-death struggle between the forces of good and evil, between God and Satan. And for people like you and me, it can feel overwhelming.

Do you sometimes feel like we're caught in this struggle? Like there are powerful forces at work in the world and we're powerless in the face of them? I think each of us has experienced that struggle in one form or another. Where do you feel caught between powerful forces? Is it a global issue like world hunger or global warming? Is it a national struggle like deconstructing racist systems? Maybe your struggle hits closer to home. Maybe for you the most powerful forces pulling at you are deciding what to do with your aging parents. Or facing mental illness, addictions, or chronic pain. Or how to survive in a workplace that seems to demand more and more and give less and less.

Or maybe you're a young person in school, and the forces are all the expectations of your parents and your sports teams and your friends and how you're going to balance it all. Or maybe you're caught between two parents who are pulling at you in opposite directions, and you just don't know what to do.

You see, the struggles are everywhere. We each find ourselves caught in situations with so much at stake, and we're not sure how we're going to make it through. Quite frankly, we don't know how it's going to end.

John of Patmos didn't know how things would end, either. He has witnessed so much struggle. But in this vision, he suddenly sees the holy city of Jerusalem where people are now able to live in safety and harmony with the natural world around them. Then he recognizes the Tree of Life from the book of Genesis. He notices that it bears not just one kind of fruit but twelve! He hears a voice saying that "the leaves of the Tree are for the healing of the nations." He thinks about all the problems in the world, the struggles, the persecution. He knows that this tree and its leaves were meant for those problems, to heal all of those ills, to reconcile all those wrongs. Then he sees that there is another tree not far away, and another, and another. There is not just one Tree of Life, but twelve of them lining the banks on both sides of the river. Twelve is a perfect number in the Bible, so the fact that there are twelve trees bearing twelve different kinds of fruit tells us just how perfect God's realm is.

John's eyes follow the river upstream and he is in awe at what he sees. The river has a surprise ending! Or rather, a surprise beginning! It's the most spectacular sight he's ever beheld. It is the throne of God! It is made of gold and precious jewels of all colors of the rainbow, yet it is transparent as glass. He sees water flowing directly from the throne, cascading down in a magnificent waterfall.

But here's the key. At the center of the Throne of God—in the very nucleus of God's realm—is *the Lamb,* meaning Jesus, the crucified one. Jesus was caught in that struggle, too. It was a life-and-death battle between forces that seemed bigger than him. And that struggle pulled at him, pounded the nails through his flesh, pushed the air from his lungs, swallowed him up in death's grip.

The cross concentrates everything that is wrong with this world. All the sin, all the violence, all the corruption, all the war, all the hunger, all the inequality and racism and sexism and classism—it all converges here. But God takes this symbol of death and pulls it inside out, transforms it into the symbol for new life.

You want to see the throne of God? Then you have to focus your eyes here on the cross, because the Lamb *is* the throne of God! Do you remember what happened when Jesus' side was pierced? Blood and water flowed from his side. Communion and baptism. The body of Christ and the river of life flowing from the throne of God.

A light radiates from the throne of God and infuses everything John sees. Then he hears the voice of God: "See, I am coming soon! Come! Let everyone who is thirsty come. Let anyone who wishes take the water of life as a gift. Surely I am coming soon."

You see, Revelation is not meant to be some pie-in-the-sky portrait of a dreamland utopia far removed from our daily lives and current struggles. John's vision is intended to give courage and hope to the church, to you and me. This vision relates directly to the struggle for justice in which we are engaged in order to bring about God's new world.

God intends for churches to be the Trees of Life, and their members are the leaves that are meant for the healing of the nations. We are planted beside the river of life. The water from that river is absorbed by us, by our churches, by other communities and organizations around the world that work for God's purposes. We are the ones to bear that fruit and offer those leaves of healing.

When you are in the midst of that struggle, when you find yourself caught between forces bigger than you that threaten to overwhelm you and break you down, you need to remember that you are planted by that river. The church is like a living tree, planted by crystal-clear water that will never fail us. It will never grow stagnant, and it will never run dry because that river flows from the throne of God, flows from the Lamb. We know that the life-giving river of Jesus can sustain us in the midst of the struggle, nourish us when we're feeling parched, strengthen us when we're pulled by forces that threaten our very lives.

Shall we gather at the river? Yes, we'll gather at the river. Join me in this call and response: Shall we gather at the river? *Yes, we'll gather at the river.*

["Shall We Gather" hymn begins playing softly in background.]

Shall we gather at the river? *Yes, we'll gather at the river.* We gather at the river with Pharaoh's daughter and the mother and sister of Moses to rescue a baby from death, confident that God's love will bring out the best in people.

Shall we gather at the river? *Yes, we'll gather at the river.* We gather with the people of Israel as they cross the waters parted by Moses, confident that God will provide for us in our times of deepest despair.

Shall we gather at the river? *Yes, we'll gather at the river.* We gather at the Jordan River with the Israelites ready to cross over to the Promised Land, confident that the river can bring us back to God.

Shall we gather at the river? *Yes, we'll gather at the river.* We gather at the river with Ezekiel in the midst of the Exile, seeing the river flowing with clean, clear water, healing our ravaged earth, confident that God's river can bring new life.

Shall we gather at the river? *Yes, we'll gather at the river.* We gather at the river with John of Patmos, drinking in that crystal-clear, life-giving water that will cleanse us and give birth to a new world with trees for the healing of the nations.

Shall we gather at the river? *Yes, we'll gather at the river.* The beautiful, the beautiful river. Gather with the saints at the river that flows from the throne of God.[8] Come Lord Jesus. Amen! Let us sing! *[Congregation sings hymn, "Shall We Gather at the River."]*

---

8. Lowry, "Shall We Gather at the River?"

Bibliography

Allen, Ronald J. *I Will Tell You the Mystery: A Commentary for Preaching*. Eugene, OR: Cascade, 2019.
Bailey, Sarah Pulliam. "'I am the chosen one': Trump again plays on messianic claims as he embraces 'King of Israel.'" *The Washington Post*, August 21, 2019. https://www.washingtonpost.com/religion/2019/08/21/i-am-chosen-one-trump-again-plays-messianic-claims-he-embraces-king-israel-title/.
Bird, Brad, dir. *Tomorrowland*. Walt Disney Studios, 2015.
Blount, Brian K. *Revelation: A Commentary*, NTL. Louisville: Westminster John Knox, 2009.
Bonhoeffer, Dietrich. *The Cost of Discipleship*. London: SCM, 1937.
Borger, Julian. "'Brought to Jesus': the evangelical grip on the Trump administration." *The Guardian*, January 11, 2019. https://www.theguardian.com/us-news/2019/jan/11/trump-administration-evangelical-influence-support.
Boring, M. Eugene. *Revelation*. Louisville: Westminster John Knox, 1989.
Brueggemann, Walter. *Money and Possessions*. Interpretation: Resources for the Use of Scripture in the Church. Louisville: Westminster John Knox, 2016.
Buechner, Frederick. *Beyond Words: Daily Readings in the ABC's of Faith*. San Francisco: HarperSanFrancisco, 2004.
Dinnerstein, Dorothy. "Survival on Earth: The Meaning of Feminism." In *Healing the Wounds: The Promise of Ecofeminism*, edited by Judith Plant, 192–200. Philadelphia: New Society, 1989.
Duffer, Matt, and Ross Duffer, dirs. *Stranger Things*, Season 1. Netflix, 2016.
Eliade, Mircea. *The Myth of the Eternal Return*. New York: Bollingen Foundation, 1954.
Eslinger, Richard L. *The Web of Preaching: New Options in Homiletical Method*. Nashville: Abingdon, 2002.
Friedman, Thomas L. *Hot, Flat, and Crowded : Why We Need a Green Revolution—and How It Can Renew America*. New York: Farrar, Straus and Giroux, 2008.
Gore, Albert. *Earth in the Balance: Ecology and the Human Spirit*. Boston: Houghton Mifflin, 1992.
Jensen, Derrick. *A Language Older Than Words*. New York: Context, 2000.
Keller, Catherine. *Apocalypse Now and Then: A Feminist Guide to the End of the World*. Boston: Beacon, 1996.
———. *Face of the Deep : A Theology of Becoming*. New York: Routledge, 2003.
LaHaye, Tim, and Jerry B. Jenkins. *Left Behind: A Novel of Earth's Last Days*. Wheaton, IL: Tyndale, 1995.

Bibliography

Lischer, Richard. *A Theology of Preaching: The Dynamics of the Gospel*. Rev. ed. Eugene, OR: Wipf and Stock, 2001.

Lord, Jennifer. *Finding Language and Imagery: Words for Holy Speech*. Elements of Preaching. Minneapolis: Fortress, 2009.

Lowry, Eugene. *The Homiletical Plot: The Sermon as Narrative Art Form*. Expanded ed. Louisville: Westminster John Knox, 2001.

Lowry, Robert. "Shall We Gather at the River?" Hymn. 1864. Public domain.

McClure, John S. *Other-Wise Preaching: A Postmodern Ethic for Homiletics*. St. Louis: Chalice, 2001.

McKinley, Jesse. "The only rapture was in the anticipation." *Philadelphia Inquirer*, May 22, 2011.

Metzger, Bruce. *Breaking the Code: Understanding the Book of Revelation*. Nashville: Abingdon, 1993.

Ngien, Dennis. "Theology of Preaching in Martin Luther." *Themelios* 28.2 (2003) 28–48. http://www.biblicalstudies.org.uk/pdf/themelios/luther_ngien.pdf).

Norris, Kathleen. *Introduction to Revelation*. Pocket Canon Series. New York: Grove, 1999.

Now This News. "Trump's Faith Advisor Paula White Is Now a White House Staffer." November 5, 2019. https://www.youtube.com/watch?v=5wokSkvusjI.

Plumer, Brad. "Scientists made a detailed 'roadmap' for meeting the Paris climate goals. It's eye-opening." Vox.com, March 24, 2017. https://www.vox.com/energy-and-environment/2017/3/23/15028480/roadmap-paris-climate-goals. Accessed Nov. 28, 2019.

Quanbeck, Philip A. II. "Preaching Apocalyptic Texts." *Word & World* 25 (2005) 317–27.

Rockström, Johan, Owen Gaffney, Joeri Rogelj, Malte Meinshausen, Nebojsa Nakicenovic, Hans and Joachim Schellnhuber. "A roadmap for rapid decarbonization." *Science* 355.6331 (March 24, 2017) 1269–71.

Rossing, Barbara R. *The Rapture Exposed: The Message of Hope in the Book of Revelation*. New York: Basic, 2004.

———. "The World is About to Turn: Preaching, Apocalyptic Texts for a Planet in Peril." In *Eco-Reformation: Grace and Hope for a Planet in Peril*, edited by Lisa E. Dahill and Jim B. Martin-Schramm, 140–59. Eugene, OR: Cascade, 2016.

Santmire, H. Paul. *The Travail of Nature: The Ambiguous Ecological Promise of Christian Theology*. Philadelphia: Fortress, 1985.

Schade, Leah D. *For the Beauty of the Earth: A Lenten Devotional*. St. Louis: Chalice, 2019.

Sheppard, Phillis-Isabella, Ronald J. Allen, and Dawn Ottoni-Wilhelm, eds. *Preaching Prophetic Care: Building Bridges to Justice, Essays in Honor of Dale P. Andrews*. Eugene, OR: Wipf and Stock, 2018.

Sisters of Notre Dame de Namur. "Expanded Story of Sister Dorothy Stang." https://www.sndohio.org/sister-dorothy/expanded-story.

Sleeth, Matthew. *Reforesting Faith: What Trees Teach Us About God and His Love for Us*. New York: Waterbrook, 2019.

Small, Fred. "Praise Be the Flood." In *Rooted and Rising: Voices of Courage in a Time of Climate Crisis*, edited by Leah D. Schade and Margaret Bullitt-Jonas, 31–36. Lanham, MD: Rowman & Littlefield, 2019.

Stroud, Dean G. *Preaching in Hitler's Shadow: Sermons of Resistance in the Third Reich*. Grand Rapids: Eerdmans, 2013.

Sumney, Jerry L. *Steward of God's Mysteries: Paul and Early Church Tradition*. Grand Rapids: Eerdmans, 2017.

Bibliography

Sumney, Jerry L., and Larry Paul Jones. *Preaching Apocalyptic Texts*. Preaching Classic Texts. St. Louis: Chalice, 1999.

Swedish, Margaret. *Living Beyond the "End of the World": A Spirituality of Hope*. Maryknoll, NY: Orbis, 2008.

Symeon the New Theologian. In *The Enlightened Heart: An Anthology of Sacred Poetry*, edited by Stephen Mitchell. New York: Harper and Row, 1989.

Thomas, Cal. "Does Trump need spiritual adviser Paula White-Cain?" *Washington Times*, November 6, 2019. https://www.washingtontimes.com/news/2019/nov/6/does-trump-need-spiritual-adviser-paula-white-cain/. Accessed Jan. 13, 2020

Walker, Barbara G. *The Woman's Dictionary of Symbols and Sacred Objects*. San Francisco: HarperSanFrancisco, 1988.

Wallace-Wells, David. *The Uninhabitable Earth: Life After Warming*. New York: Tim Duggan, 2019.

Whyte, David. *What to Remember When Waking*. Sounds True audiobook. N. p.: 2010.

Wink, Walter. *Engaging the Powers: Discernment and Resistance in a World of Domination*. Philadelphia: Fortress, 1993.

Wong, Edward. "The Rapture and the Real World: Mike Pompeo Blends Beliefs and Policy." *New York Times*, March 30, 2019. https://www.nytimes.com/2019/03/30/us/politics/pompeo-christian-policy.html.

World Bank, The. "Poverty Overview." October 2, 2019. https://www.worldbank.org/en/topic/poverty/overview.

Wuellner, Flora Slosson. "A Broken Piece of Barley Bread" *Weavings* 14.6 (November/December 2004) 7–9.

www.ingramcontent.com/pod-product-compliance
Lightning Source LLC
Chambersburg PA
CBHW031433150426
43191CB00006B/495